Ultimate Floral CROSS STITCH

INDEX

Ultimate Floral CROSS STITCH

Jane Alford ● Angela Beazley ● Sue Cook ● Angela Davidson
Christina Marsh ● Denise Roberts ● Elena Thomas ● Shirley Watts

INDEX

THE CHARTS

Some of the designs in this book are very detailed and, due to inevitable space limitations, the charts may be shown on a comparatively small scale; in such cases, readers may find it helpful to have the particular chart with which they are currently working enlarged.

THREADS

The projects in this book were all stitched with DMC, Anchor or Madeira stranded cotton embroidery threads. The keys given with each chart also list thread combinations for all three types of thread. It should be pointed out that the shades produced by different companies vary slightly, and it is not always possible to find identical colours in a different range.

Due to the difficulty of true photograph colour reproduction, the threads recommended do not always match the photographs exactly.

This edition published in 1999 for INDEX
Index Books Ltd. Henson Way, Kettering NN16 8PX

Published in 1999 by Merehurst Limited
Ferry House, 51–57 Lacy Road, Putney, London SW15 1PR

Text on pp 48, 50–51, 54–55, 81–83, 169–171, 193–195, 205–207, 217–219, 221–223, 229–231, 237–239, 248, 250–251 ©Copyright Jane Alford 1999
Text on pp 12, 14–15, 21–23, 44, 46–47, 64, 66–67, 108, 110–111, 136, 138–139, 141–143, 185–187, 196, 198–199 ©Copyright Shirley Watts 1999
All other text ©Copyright Merehurst Limited 1999
Photography and illustrations ©Copyright Merehurst Limited 1999

ISBN 1 85391 856 3

Edited and Designed by Axis Design
Commissioning Editor: Karen Hemingway
Project Editor: Angela Newton
Publishing Manager: Fia Fornari
Production Manager: Lucy Byrne
CEO & Publisher: Anne Wilson
Marketing & Sales Director: Kathryn Harvey
International Sales Director: Kevin Lagden

Photography by Marie-Louise Avery (pp 100–101, 136–137, 140–141, 184–185,196–197)
Debbie Patterson (pp 28–29, 36–37, 48–49, 52–53, 80–81, 168–169, 192–193, 204–205, 216–217, 220–221, 228–229, 236–237, 248–249)
Juliet Piddington (pp 16–17, 24–25, 32–33, 40–41, 56–57, 60–61, 68–69, 72–73, 76–77, 84–85, 88–89, 92–93, 96–97, 104–105, 114–115, 118–119, 120–121, 124–125, 128–129, 132–133, 144–145, 148–149, 152–153, 156–157, 160–161, 164–165, 172–173, 176–177, 180–181, 188–189, 200–201, 208–209, 212–213, 224–225, 232–233, 240–241, 244–245, 252–253)
Illustrations by John Hutchinson
Colour separation by Colourscan
Printed by Tien Wah Press in Singapore

Merehurst is the leading publisher of craft books and has an excellent range of titles to suit all levels.
Please send to the address above for our free catalogue, stating the title of this book.

❀ Contents ❀

INTRODUCTION

Cross stitch is such a simple and venerable form of embroidery, and flowers are such a universal decorative motif, that it is no wonder that floral cross stitch patterns are so enduringly popular. This book presents an inspiring collection of floral projects, from simple motifs for decorating greetings cards to more challenging designs for framed pictures or cushions that will take pride of place in your living room. There are projects for decorating household linen and clothes, but also for items such as clothes brushes, coasters and trinkets boxes, all available from specialist suppliers, in which you can mount your embroidery.

Roses are well represented here, of course, but tulips, nasturtiums, daffodils, irises, pansies, sunflowers, lavender, daisies, hydrangeas, periwinkles and honeysuckle are also featured. With so many designs to choose from, there is sure to be one that includes your favourite flower. There are also some more unusual designs, such as the desktop set with its Art Nouveau-style topiary trees, or the stationery items featuring herb designs in combined cross-stitch and Assisi work.

There are designs in this book to suit the novice as well as those to help keep the most skilled embroiderer busy. Some of the designs are stitched on easy-to-sew Aida fabric, which is ideal for beginners, but if you prefer to work on linen for a more traditional finish, you can substitute the 14-count Aida with a 28-count evenweave, taking each stitch over two fabric threads.

Many of the designs can easily be adapted for other items – a design for a bookmark can be repeated in several lengths to form a cake band, for example, or the pretty poppy nightdress case could easily be adapted to make an attractive herbal sleep pillow. Browse through the book and you will soon come up with plenty of other ideas for projects to suit your own particular requirements.

The first chapter, *Quick and Easy Treasures*, includes a range of easy projects that can all be completed in just a couple of hours and make ideal small gift items. *Cosy Cushions* features traditional and more vibrant designs to brighten up your living room. Work one of the projects from *Floral Greetings* for a friend or loved one's special day, and your good wishes will be treasured long after the event. Flowers make a thoroughly feminine bedroom, and you will find an enchanting array of suitable bedroom accessories in the chapter on *Boudoir Trinkets*, including jewellery boxes and pot pourri sachets. *Luxury Linens* carries the floral theme throughout the rest of the house, with delectable tablecloths, beautiful place mats and even a hydrangea tea cosy. Finally, cross stitch is elevated from decoration to a work of art in its own right in the *Pictures and Samplers* chapter with a selection of traditional and more unusual samplers

A *Basic Skills* section clearly explains how to prepare your fabric, use an embroidery hoop and work the basic stitches, as well as how to finish and mount your work for display. Whatever your level of sewing skill, with this book you will soon be creating beautiful things to charm and delight all who see them.

BASIC TECHNIQUES

PREPARING THE FABRIC

Even with an average amount of handling, even-weave fabrics tend to fray at the edges, so it is a good idea to overcast the raw edges, using ordinary sewing thread, before you begin. Alternatively, wrap masking tape over the edges.

FABRIC

Some projects use Aida fabric, which is ideal for beginners and more advanced stitchers as it has a surface of clearly designated squares. Aida fabric has a count, which refers to the number of squares (each stitch covers one square) to 2.5cm (1in); the higher the count, the smaller the finished stitching.

Other projects use either 14- or 18-count Aida, popular and readily available sizes, in a wide variety of colours. Linen has been used for several projects in this book; although less simple to stitch on than Aida (because you need to count over a specified number of threads) it gives a very attractive, finish. The most commonly available linen has 28 threads to 2.5cm (1in), which when worked over two threads gives a stitch count of 14 to 2.5cm (1in).

THE INSTRUCTIONS

Each project begins with a full list of the materials that you will require. Aida, Tula, Lugana and Linda are all fabrics produced by Zmeigart. Note that the measurements given for the embroidery fabric include a minimum of 3cm (1½in) all around to allow for stretching into a frame and preparing the edges to prevent them from fraying.

Colour keys for stranded embroidery cottons – DMC, Anchor, or Madeira – are given with each chart. You will need to buy one skein of each colour mentioned in a key, though you may use less. If two or more skeins are needed, this is stated. You may also find it helpful to enlarge the charts.

Before you begin to embroider, mark the centre of the design with two lines of basting stitches, one vertical and one horizontal, running from edge to edge of the fabric, as indicated by the arrows on the charts. Use the centre lines on the chart and these basting threads on the fabric as reference points for counting the squares and threads to position the design.

ENLARGING A GRAPH PATTERN

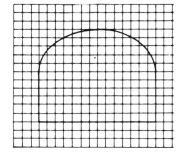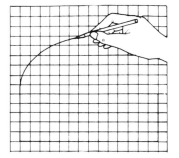

To enlarge a graph pattern, you will need a sheet of graph paper ruled in 1cm (⅜in) squares, a ruler and pencil. If, for example, the scale is one square to 5cm (2in) mark the appropriate lines to give a grid of the correct size. Copy the graph freehand from the small grid to the larger one, completing one square at a time. Use a ruler to draw the straight lines first, then copy the freehand curves.

WORKING IN A HOOP

A hoop is the most popular frame for use with small areas of embroidery. It consists of two rings, one fitted inside the other; the outer ring usually has an adjustable screw attachment so that it can be tightened to hold the stretched fabric in place. Embroidery hoops are readily available in several sizes, ranging from 10cm (4in) in diameter to quilting hoops with a diameter of 38cm (15in). Hoops with table stands or floor stands attached are also available.

To stretch your fabric in a hoop, place the area to be embroidered over the inner ring and press the outer ring over it, with the tension screw released. Tissue paper can be placed between the outer ring and the embroidery, so that the hoop does not mark the fabric. Lay the tissue paper over the fabric when you set it in the hoop, then tear away the central embroidery area. If the fabric creases, release the outer hoop and try again. Smooth the fabric and, if necessary, straighten the grain before tightening the screw. The fabric should be evenly stretched.

WORKING IN A RECTANGULAR FRAME

Rectangular frames are more suitable for larger pieces of embroidery. They consist of two rollers, with tapes attached, and two flat side pieces, which slot into the rollers and are held in place by pegs or screw attachments. Available in different sizes, frames are measured by the length of the roller tape, ranging from 30cm (12in) to 68cm (27in).

As alternatives to a slate frame, canvas stretchers and the backs of old picture frames can be used. Provided there is sufficient extra fabric around the finished size of the embroidery, the edges of the fabric can be turned under and simply attached to the sides of the frame with drawing pins (thumb tacks) or staples.

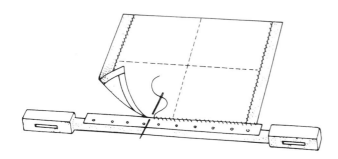

1 To stretch your fabric in a rectangular frame, cut out the fabric, allowing at least an extra 5cm (2m) all around the finished size of the embroidery. Baste a single 12mm (½in) turning on the top and bottom edges and oversew strong tape, 2.5cm (1in) wide, to the other two sides. Mark the centre line on the fabric both ways with large basting stitches. Working from the centre outwards and using a needle and strong thread, oversew the top and bottom edges to the roller tapes. Fit the side pieces into the slots, and roll any extra fabric on one roller until the fabric is completely taut.

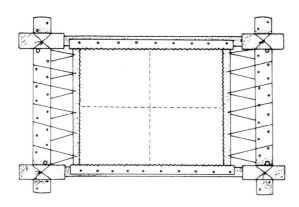

2 Insert the pegs or adjust the screw attachment to secure the frame. Thread a large-eyed needle (chenille needle) with strong thread or fine string and lace both edges of the fabric, securing the ends around the intersections of the frame. Lace the webbing at 2.5cm (1in) intervals, stretching the fabric evenly.

EXTENDING EMBROIDERY FABRIC

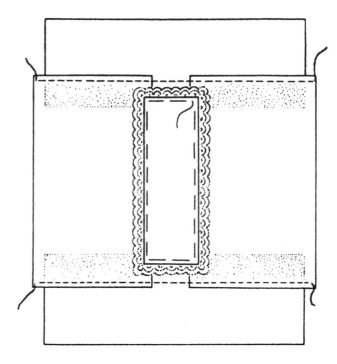

It is easy to extend a piece of embroidery fabric, such as a bookmark, to stretch it in a hoop. Fabric oddments of a similar weight can be used. Simply cut four pieces to size (in other words, to the measurement that will fit both the embroidery fabric and your hoop) and baste them to each side of the embroidery fabric before stretching it in the hoop in the usual way.

WORKING WITH WASTE CANVAS

Waste canvas provides a removable grid over which you can stitch on unevenly-woven fabrics. Once the design has been stitched, the canvas is removed. Determine the size of the design, and cut a piece of canvas that allows a border of at least 5cm (2in) all around.

Baste the waste canvas to the design area of the fabric/item you are using. Stitch your design in the usual way, making sure it is centred on the fabric/item. When stitching is complete, remove the basting stitches and lightly dampen the canvas with water.

When stitching is complete, remove the basting stitches. Then lightly dampen the canvas with water. Slowly and gently pull out the threads of canvas, one at a time, using a pair of tweezers. Take great care and do not hurry this process, because hasty work could result in spoiling your stitching. You may need to re-dampen stubborn threads that will not pull out.

SEWING TECHNIQUES

CROSS STITCH

For all cross stitch embroidery, the following two methods of working are used. Each produces neat rows of stitches on the back of the fabric.

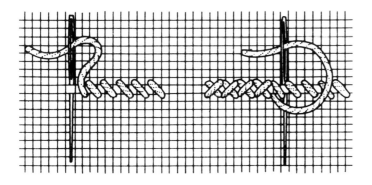

When stitching large areas of one colour, such as a background, it is easiest to work in horizontal rows. Working from right to left, complete the first row of evenly spaced diagonal stitches over the number of threads specified in the project instructions. Then, working from left to right, repeat. Continue in this way to fill the area, making sure each stitch crosses in the same direction.

When stitching diagonal lines, work downwards, completing each stitch before moving to the next. Make sure all the crosses look the same, with the top of the cross going in the same direction. Begin to embroider at the centre of the design and work outwards.

THREE-QUARTER CROSS STITCH

Fractional stitches are used on certain projects. When making a fractional stitch, should you find it difficult to pierce the centre of the Aida block, try using a sharp needle to make a small hole in the centre first, before making the stitch.

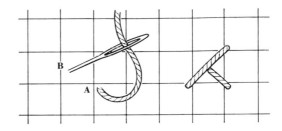

To work a three-quarter cross, bring the needle up at point A and down through the centre of the square at B. Later, the diagonal back stitch finishes the stitch. A chart square with two different symbols separated by a diagonal line requires two 'three-quarter' stitches. Backstitch will later finish the square.

A three-quarter stitch occupies half of a square diagonally. A half cross stitch is like a normal cross stitch, but only the top diagonal stitch is worked, to give a more delicate effect to the finished design. Stitches worked in this way are indicated quite clearly on the colour keys.

BACKSTITCH

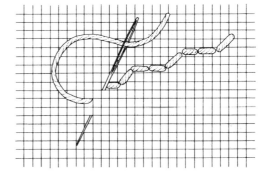

Backstitch is used to emphasize a particular fold-line, an outline or a shadow. The stitches are worked over the same number of threads as the cross stitch, forming continuous lines.

Make the first stitch from left to right; pass the needle behind the fabric and bring it out one stitch length ahead to the left. Repeat and continue in this way along the line.

FRENCH KNOTS

This stitch is shown on some of the diagrams by a small dot. Where there are several French knots featured in the design, the dots have been omitted from the diagrams to avoid confusion. Where this occurs you should refer to the instructions of the project and the colour photograph.

To work a French knot, bring your needle and cotton out slightly to the right of where you want your knot to be. Wind the thread once or twice around the needle, depending on how big you want your knot to be, and insert the needle to the left of the point where you brought it out. However, do not pull too hard or the knot will disappear through the fabric.

TENT STITCH

Tent stitch is worked diagonally over only one intersection of the canvas and the needle always covers at least two threads on the reverse side of the work. It looks similar to half cross stitch from the front of the stitching, but from the back it produces long sloping stitches whereas half cross stitch has vertical stitches.

To work tent stitch, start at the top right and work from right to left. Start with the needle behind the fabric, bring it out through a square, then take it diagonally over one intersection to the upper right. Then bring it out in the square to the left of the first stitch and take it down diagonally over one intersection to the upper right. Continue across the fabric in the same way.

METALLIC THREADS AND BLENDING

You should use no more than 45cm (18in) of thread at a time. Double the thread about 5cm (2in) at one end, and inset the loop through the eye of the needle. Pull the loop over the point of the needle and gently pull the loop towards the end of the eye to secure the thread to the needle. If you are combining blending filament and stranded cotton, thread the latter through the eye in the usual way, and clip it to match the length of the blending filament.

SPECIALIST THREADS

Both silky blending filaments and metallic braids are used in some of these projects. Some require the blending filament to be blended with stranded cotton while in others it is used singly. For ease of working with blending filament, slightly dampen the thread before knotting it into the needle and then threading on the stranded cotton (not suitable for metallic threads). Metallic braids and blending filament should only be used in short lengths to prevent tangling and to stop the fibres 'stripping' off as the thread is pulled through the fabric.

ATTACHING BEADS

Some projects in this book use beads to add interest. These are either represented by a symbol on the chart or full description of the beads will be listed in the instructions. Beading needles are available but are often very fine and difficult to handle. A No26 tapestry needle will pass through the eye of most seed beads and they are normally attached when the rest of the stitching is complete. Stitch on using a half cross stitch from upper left to lower right, finishing off securely.

MITRING A CORNER

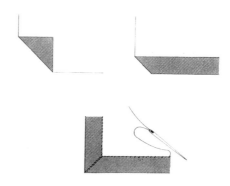

Press a single hem to the wrong side, the same as the measurement given in the instructions. Open the hem out again and fold the corner of the fabric inwards as shown on the diagram. Refold the hem to the reverse side along the pressed line, and slip-stitch in place.

BINDING AN EDGE

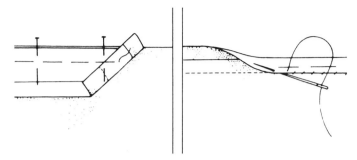

1 Open out the turning on one edge of the bias binding and pin in position on the right side of the fabric, matching the fold to the seamline. Fold over the cut end of the binding. Finish the binding by overlapping the starting point by about 12mm (½in). Baste and then machine stitch along the seamline to secure.

2 Fold the binding over the raw edge to the wrong side. Then baste to secure and, using matching sewing thread, neatly hem the binding in place and press.

PIPED SEAMS

You can cover piping cord with either bias-cut fabric of your choice or a bias binding; alternatively, ready-covered piping cord is available in several widths and many colours.

1 To apply piping, pin and baste it to the right side of the fabric, with seam lines matching. Clip into the seam allowance where necessary and trim excess fabric.

2 With right sides together, place the second piece of fabric on top, enclosing the piping inside. Baste and then hand or machine stitch using a zip foot. Stitch as close to the piping as possible, covering the first line of stitching.

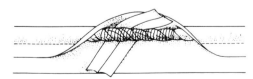

3 To join ends of piping cord, overlap the two ends by 2.5cm (1in). Unpick the two cut ends of bias to reveal the cord. Join the bias strip as shown. Trim and press the seam open. Unravel and splice the two ends of the cord. Fold the bias over it, and finish basting around the edge.

MOUNTING EMBROIDERY

The cardboard should be cut to the size of the finished embroidery, with an extra 6mm (¼in) added all round to allow for the recess in the frame.

LIGHTWEIGHT FABRICS

Place embroidery face down, with the cardboard centred on top, and basting and pencil lines matching. Fold over the fabric at each corner and secure with masking tape. Fold over the fabric on each side, securing it firmly with pieces of masking tape about 2.5cm (1in) apart. Neaten the mitred corners with masking tape, pulling the fabric tightly.

HEAVIER FABRICS

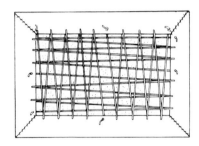

Lay the embroidery face down, with the cardboard centred on top; fold over the edges of the fabric on opposite sides, making mitred folds at the corners, and lace across, using strong thread. Repeat on the other two sides. Finally, pull up the stitches fairly tightly to stretch the fabric firmly over the cardboard. Overstitch the mitred corners.

USING PERFORATED PAPER

Perforated paper will give a finished piece of embroidery the same size as a piece stitched on 14-count Aida fabric. Use three strands of embroidery thread and cut the paper 5cm (2in) larger all round than your design to make it easier to handle.

A cross stitch is stitched between four of the holes on the paper. Handle the paper carefully and pull the thread smoothly through the holes. If the paper tears repair it with a small piece of sticky tape on the reverse side. If the chart you are using has been designed for perforated paper, it will include a cutting line, otherwise cut vertically, horizontally and diagonally around your embroidery when finished. Leave at least one square between the edge and the design so that the stitches do not come out.

Quick and Easy Treasures

A couple of hours is all you need for these simple projects. So if you're new to cross stitch and want a project that's not too taxing, or you're just short of time, these are for you.

FLOWERS IN OVAL FRAMES

YOU WILL NEED

For each Flower Picture, mounted in an oval portrait frame, with an aperture measuring 14cm x 9.5cm (5½in x 3¾in):

20cm x 15cm (8in x 6in) of cream, 18-count Aida fabric
Stranded embroidery cotton in the colours given in the panel
No26 tapestry needle
Strong thread for lacing across the back when mounting
Stiff cardboard for mounting
Frame of your choice

•

THE EMBROIDERY

For each picture, prepare the fabric, marking the centre lines of the design with basting stitches. Start your embroidery from the centre of the design, completing the cross stitching first, and then the backstitching. Use two strands of thread for both the cross stitch and the backstitching, except when outlining the laburnum flowers, for which one strand is used. Gently steam press the finished embroidery on the reverse side.

ASSEMBLING THE PICTURE

Each picture is assembled in the same way. Trim the edges of the embroidery until it measures 19cm x 14cm (7½in x 5½in) and centre the picture over the cardboard mounting. Lace the embroidery over the mount, following the instructions in *Basic Skills* pages 8–11, and complete the assembly according to the manufacturer's instructions.

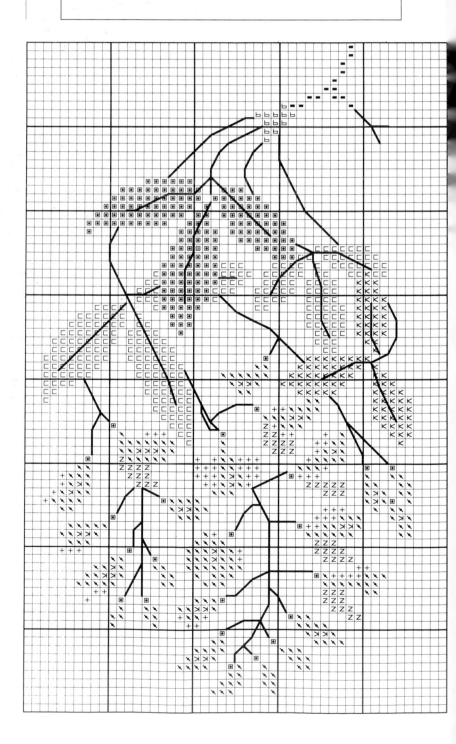

▼ LABURNUM		DMC	ANCHOR	MADEIRA
▬	Brown	610	889	2106
Z	Deep yellow	444	291	0105
◤	Yellow	307	289	0104
C	Dark green	3362	862	1601
▭	Pale green	472	264	1414
⊡	Green	3347	266	1408
K	Light green	3348	265	1409
+	Yellow green	734	279	1610
◥	Lemon	445	288	0103

Note: Backstitch twig in brown, the stems of the two dark leaves and the vein of the leaf worked in green in dark green, and all other stems and leaves in green.

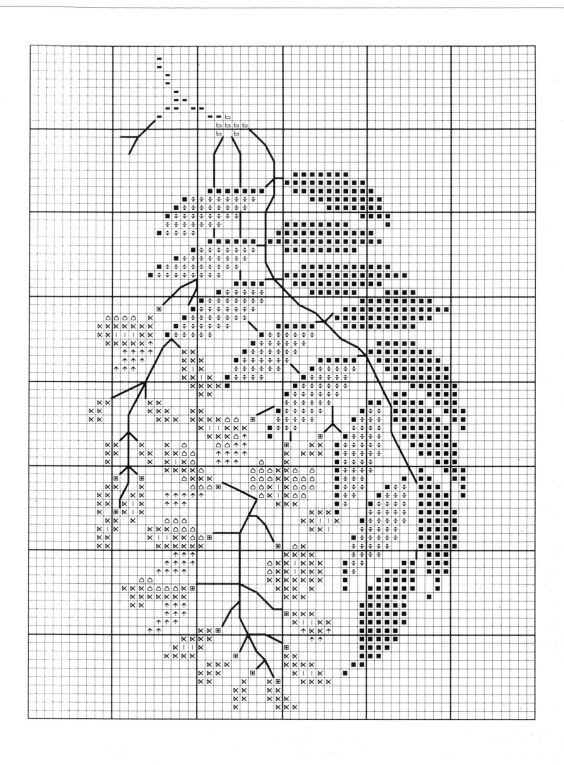

▲ WISTARIA				
		DMC	ANCHOR	MADEIRA
▬	Brown	610	889	2106
ㅂ	Pale green	472	264	1414
■	Dark green	3346	817	1407
◉	Green	3347	266	1408
÷	Yellowy green	470	267	1502
△	Dull mauve	3041	871	0806
↑	Deep mauve	208	110	0804
⋈	Mauve	210	108	0802
I	Pale mauve	211	342	0801

Note: Backstitch the twig in brown and all other stalks in green.

Floral Cottages

These little cottages are colourful and quick to complete. The versatile designs are shown stitched as small pictures and as bread cloths to enhance baskets of bread for the table. The designs could also be used for greeting cards.

FLORAL COTTAGES

YOU WILL NEED

For each Picture, with a design area of 7.5cm (3in) square:

25cm (10in) square of pale blue, 14-count Aida fabric
Stranded embroidery cotton in the colours given
in the panel
No24 and No26 tapestry needles
Cardboard and masking tape
Frame of your choice

For each Bread Cloth, with a design area of 7cm (2¾in) square:

33cm (13in) square of ivory, 28-count evenweave fabric
Stranded embroidery cotton in the colours given
in the panel
No24 and No26 tapestry needles
Cream stranded embroidery cotton

●

THE PICTURES

For each picture, prepare the fabric, basting horizontal and vertical lines in the fabric, following the instructions in *Basic Skills* pages 8–11. Set the fabric in a hoop and begin stitching from the centre, following the chart.

Work the cross stitch using two strands of thread in the No24 tapestry needle, stitching over one block of fabric. Make sure that all the top stitches run in the same direction. Work the backstitch using the strand of thread and the No26 needle.

When you have finished the stitching, remove the fabric from the frame. Gently hand wash the embroidery, if desired. Press on the reverse side with a warm iron. Mount the picture as shown in the *Basic Skills* pages 8–11, following the instructions for lightweight fabrics. Insert the mounted picture into the frame according to the manufacturer's instructions.

THE BREAD CLOTHS

For each cloth, prepare the fabric by measuring up 11cm (4¾in) diagonally from the bottom right corner of the fabric. This point is the centre of the chart; mark it with a pin. Set the fabric in a hoop and begin stitching from the marked point. Work the cross stitch in the same way as for the pictures, working over two threads of the fabric in each direction for a cross stitch.

When you have finished the embroidery, remove the fabric from the frame. Complete the cloth by hemstitching the edges, following the instructions for the *Cottage Garden Table Set* (page 164).

▶ FLORAL COTTAGES		ANCHOR	DMC	MADEIRA
2	White	01	Blanc	White
Z	Black	403	310	black
3	Light brick	882	3773	2313
↑	Dark brick	883	3064	2312
H	Grey	8581	646	1812
⌐	Grey blue	850	926	1707
L	Pale sand	366	739	2013
8	Sand	373	3828	2102
/	Dark sand	943	3045	2103
N	Bright brown	371	433	2303
V	Pale bright green	241	954	1211
Y	Bright green	243	912	1213
K	Medium green	267	3346	1407
S	Dark green	268	3345	1406
▼	Purple	109	210	0802
T	Red	1006	815	0511
▽	Pale yellow	293	727	0110
=	Brown	358	433	2008
	Dark brown*	381	838	1914

Note: Backstitch window detail on black and white cottage in white, and roof detail in bright brown. Backstitch window detail on other picture in dark brown (*used for backstitch only). Backstitch window details on cottages on cloths in red.*

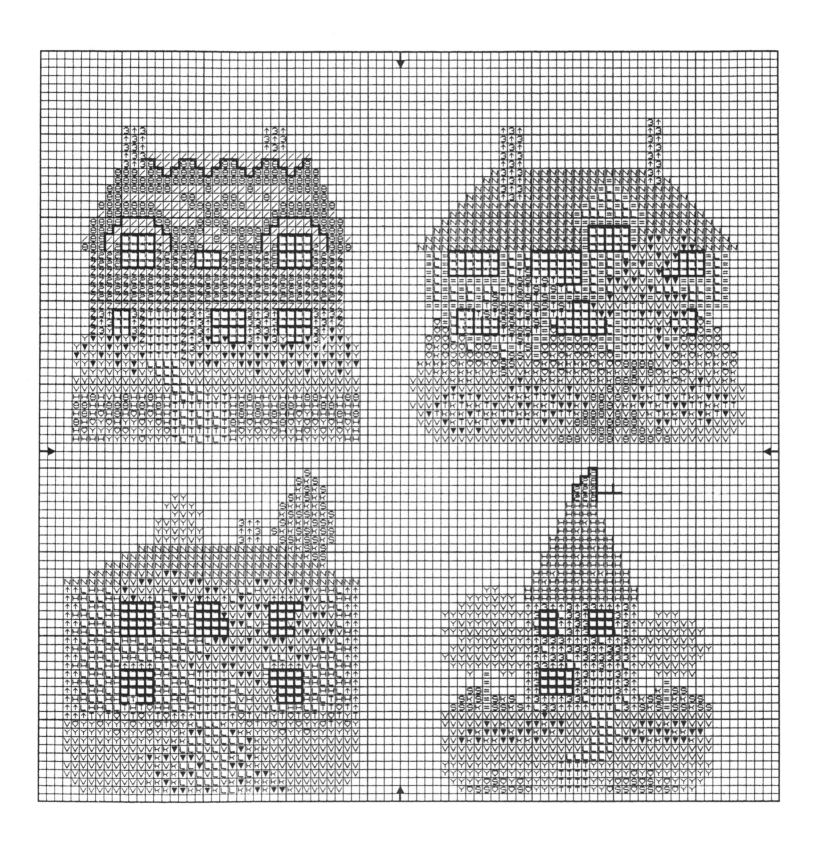

Tulip Picture

A favourite of Islamic artists and of the Dutch masters, the tulip, which originates from Asia Minor, is surely one of the most elegant and varied of cultivated flowers.
This pewter vase brim-full of striking red and yellow tulips will bring a breath of spring into your home.

Victorian Posies

Bring a touch of old-fashioned elegance to your home with this charming trio of pansy, rosebud and marigold bouquets. Their beaded bows add extra decorative interest and carry on the tradition of Victorian embroidery.

Floral Gifts

What could be more delightful than a sweet-scented sachet to place in a drawer or wardrobe, or a fragrant herb pillow to help induce sleep? These sachets are easy to make and a pleasure to receive.

FLORAL GIFTS

YOU WILL NEED

For the Dog Violet Pot Pourri Sack, measuring 9.5cm x 15.5cm (3¾in x 6¼in) approximately:

Two 14.5cm x 21cm (5¾in x 8½in) pieces of beige Hardanger fabric, Rustico, with 18 threads to 2.5cm (1in)
46cm (18in) of lilac ribbon, 12mm (½in) wide
Stranded embroidery cotton in the colours given in the appropriate panel
No26 tapestry needle
Pot pourri of your choice for filling

For the Cornflower Sachet, measuring 13cm (5in) square, excluding the lace edging:

18cm (7¼in) square of cream Aida fabric, with 18 threads to 2.5cm (1in)
15cm (6in) square of cotton net, for backing
90cm (1yd) of cream lace edging, 18mm (¾in) wide
46cm (18in) of lavender ribbon, for bow and loop
Stranded embroidery cotton in the colours given in the appropriate panel
No26 tapestry needle
Pot pourri of your choice for filling

For the Ragged Robin Herb Pillow, measuring 21.5cm x 14cm (8½in x 5½in):

Two 27cm x 19.5cm (10¾in x 7¾in) pieces of cream Aida fabric, with 18 threads to 2.5cm (1in)
70cm (27in) of cream lace edging, 18mm (¾in) wide
Stranded embroidery cotton in the colours given in the appropriate panel
No26 tapestry needle
Pot pourri of your choice for filling

THE EMBROIDERY

Prepare fabric, marking the centre lines of each design with basting stitches, with the exception of the pot pourri sack. For this, measure up 6cm (2½in) from one short edge and baste a line across from one side to the other in order to mark the base line.

Mount the fabric in a hoop or frame, (see *Basic Skills* pages 8–11). Referring to the appropriate chart, complete the cross stitching, using two strands of embroidery cotton in the needle for both the cross stitch and the backstitching. For the pot pourri sack, start from the centre of the base line. For the other designs, start from the centre and work out. Embroider the main areas first, and then finish with the backstitching. Steam press on the reverse side.

MAKING THE POT POURRI SACK

Place the two pieces of fabric with right sides together and trim to measure 11.5cm x 18cm (4½in x 7¼in). Taking a 12mm (½in) seam allowance, stitch the side and bottom seams. Roll a narrow hem around the top of the sack, stitching it by hand.

Fold the ribbon in half and, leaving a loop 5cm (2in) long at the folded end, stitch it to the side of the sack, about 3cm (1¼in) down from the top edge. Fill the sack with pot pourri and tie the ribbon securely.

MAKING THE LACE TRIMMED SACHET

Trim the embroidered fabric to measure 15cm (6in) square. With the right sides together, and taking a 12mm (½in) seam allowance, stitch it to the net, leaving an opening of 6.5cm (2½in). Trim across the corners; turn the sachet right side out and press the edges. Join the short edges of the lace with a small French seam.

Gather the lace and stitch it by hand to the edge of the sachet, allowing extra fullness at the corners. Decorate with a bow and loop of ribbon at one corner. Fill the sachet with pot pourri, and slipstitch the opening.

MAKING THE HERB PILLOW

Trim the two pieces of fabric to measure 24.5cm x 16.5cm (9½in x 6½in). With the right sides together, and taking a 12mm (½in) seam allowance, join the two pieces, leaving a gap of 8cm (3½in) in one side. Then trim across the corners; turn the pillow right side out, and press the edges. Add the lace, as for the sachet (above); then fill with pot pourri or lavender, and slipstitch the opening.

▶ DOG VIOLET

		DMC	ANCHOR	MADEIRA
—	Ecru	Ecru	926	Ecru
⊥	Pale mauve	554	97	0711
⊞	Mauve	208	110	0804
◆	Reddish orange	350	11	0213
⊘	Pale green	3364	260	1603
◆	Dark green	3345	268	1406

Note: Backstitch main stems in dark green and leaf rib in pale green.

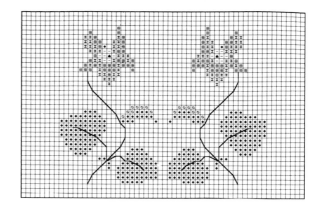

◀ CORNFLOWER

		DMC	ANCHOR	MADEIRA
❘	Pale mauve	210	108	0802
●	Light navy	336	150	1007
3	Blue	340	118	0902
▼	Dark blue	793	121	0906
↓	Green	3347	266	1408
—	Dark green	3345	268	1406

Note: Backstitch in green.

▼ RAGGED ROBIN

		DMC	ANCHOR	MADEIRA
·	Ecru	Ecru	926	Ecru
⊘	Pale pink	3609	85	0710
△	Medium pink	3608	86	0709
⊡	Deep pink	3607	87	0708
+	Pale green	3348	264	1409
	Green*	3347	266	1408
▼	Dark green	3345	268	1406
●	Purplish brown	315	896	0810

Note: Backstitch centres of two lower flowers in Ecru, and bud stalks in purplish brown, all main stems in green, and centres of five upper flowers in pale green.*

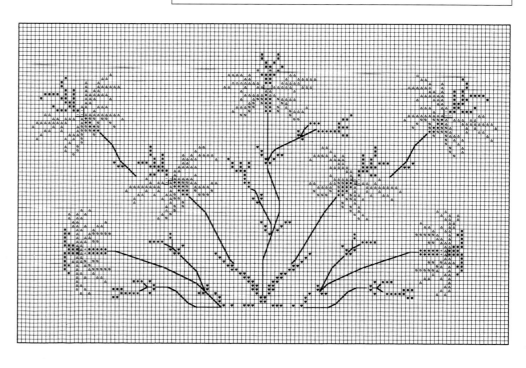

Stylized Topiary and Flowers

The classical shapes of topiary trees and stylized flowers were a recurring theme in the Art Nouveau period. These designs are especially appropriate to stitch as cards or gifts for men.

Pins and Needles

The vivid blue cornflower (*Centaurea cyanus*) provides a bold design for a pincushion. The diminutive and paler blue flowers of the forget-me-not (*Myosotis arvensis*) are used for the needlecase. These flowers have a yellow centre and are often a delicate pink in bud.

PINS AND NEEDLES

YOU WILL NEED

For the Forget-me-not Needlecase, measuring
12.5cm x 11.5cm (5in x 4½in):

33cm x 16.5cm (13in x 6½in) of cream Aida fabric,
with 18 threads to 2.5cm (1in)
27.5cm x 14cm (1in x 5½in) of satin lining fabric
25cm x 11.5cm (10in x 4½in) of heavyweight
iron-on interfacing
23cm x 9cm (9in x 3½in) of cream felt
45cm (18in) of matching ribbon, 6mm (¼in) wide
Stranded embroidery cotton in the colours given in the
appropriate panel
No26 tapestry needle

23cm (9in) square of cream Aida fabric, with 18
threads to 2.5cm (1in)
Stranded embroidery cotton in the colours given in the
appropriate panel
No26 tapestry needle
Pincushion base and pad (for suppliers, see page 256)

▼ FORGET-ME-NOT		DMC	ANCHOR	MADEIRA
Ⅰ	Yellow	307	289	0104
⬡	Pale blue	794	120	0907
T	Blue	799	145	0910
◣	Purplish blue	340	118	0902
—	Pale green	3348	264	1409
⊥	Green	3347	266	1408
+	Dark green	3346	817	1407
	Light brown*	680	901	2210

Note: Backstitch flower centres in light brown*, stems in dark green and buds in purplish blue.

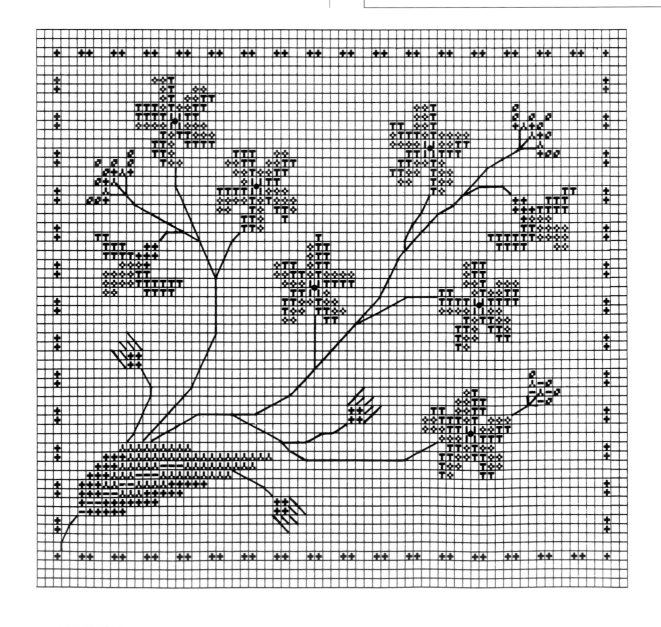

THE EMBROIDERY

For the needlecase, first fold the fabric in two, to measure 16.5cm (6½in) square. With the fold on the left, measure in 2.5cm (1in) from each raw edge and mark the upper surface of the fabric at the top, bottom and right-hand side with basting stitches. The area enclosed by the fold and basting lines is the centre of the design.

For each design, prepare the fabric and set it in a hoop (see *Basic Skills* pages 8–11). Embroider the design, using two strands of thread in the needle for both the cross stitch and the backstitching. Gently press the finished embroidery on the reverse side.

FINISHING

For the needlecase, trim the fabric to measure 27.5cm x 14cm (11in x 5½in). Make and press a 12mm (½in) turning on all sides, mitring the corners. Slide the interfacing under the turnings and iron it in place.

Turn under 12mm (½in) all around the lining and hem to cover the interfacing. Lightly stitch down the centre to attach the felt inside the case. Tie the ribbon into a bow and use to trim the spine.

For the pincushion, use a round guide to trim the fabric to a 19cm (7½in) circle. Run a line of gathering stitches around the fabric 12mm (½in) from the edge. Place over the pincushion dome and tighten until snug. Secure the thread firmly. Put the dome in the wooden base and screw firmly in place.

▼ CORNFLOWER		DMC	ANCHOR	MADEIRA
·	Pale mauve	210	108	0802
U	Light navy	336	150	1007
I	Pale blue	341	117	0901
⋰	Blue	340	118	0902
T	Dark blue	793	121	0906
◣	Green	3347	266	1408
+	Dark green	3345	268	1406

Christmas Wreaths and Garlands

Tiny wreaths and garlands are easy for beginners and perfect for decorations, cards, gift tags and many of the other small items you may need to prepare for Christmas.

Cosy Cushions

A cushion makes the ideal background for a cross stitch design, and you'll find plenty of ideas here, from a charming traditional cottage pattern to a stunning Tiffany-style iris design in vivid colours.

NASTURTIUM CUSHION

YOU WILL NEED

For the Nasturtium Cushion Cover, measuring
41cm (16in) in diameter:

46cm (18in) square of cream, 14-count Aida fabric
46cm (18in) square of cream furnishing fabric, for the
cushion back
Two 46cm (18in) squares of strong unbleached cotton
fabric, for the inner cover
Stranded embroidery cotton in the colours given
in the panel
No24 tapestry needle
3.7m (4yds) of cream cushion cord, 6mm (¼in)
in diameter
41cm (16in) cushion pad
(or cushion filling, if preferred)

•

THE EMBROIDERY

Prepare the fabric by marking the centre lines with
basting stitches. Start to embroider from the centre
of the design. Use three strands of cotton in
the needle for the cross stitch, and two strands
for the backstitch. Steam press on the reverse side
when complete.

MAKING UP THE COVER

After the embroidery is completed, use tailor's
chalk to mark a 41cm (16in) circle on both pieces
of cushion material – the Aida and the furnishing
fabric. Pin them with right sides together, and
machine around the edge, following the marked
line and leaving a 25cm (10in) opening. Trim turnings to 12mm (½in), and turn right side out.

For the inner lining to contain the cushion pad
or cushion filling, follow the same procedure.

Insert the pad or filling into the cushion lining,
and stitch up the opening. Insert the covered pad
into the embroidered cushion cover, and stitch up
the opening.

Trim the edge of the cushion with the cord, making loops at intervals, as desired; slipstitch the cord
in place.

► NASTURTIUM		DMC	ANCHOR	MADEIRA
⊥	Dark grey	844	401	1810
∷	Light grey	3022	8581	1903
·	Ecru	Ecru	926	Ecru
▬	Light orange	741	304	0201
∕	Deep yellow	972	298	0107
Z	Orange	971	316	0203
◥	Yellow	973	290	0105
‖	Bright yellow	307	289	0104
▼	Maroon	902	72	0601
▪▪	Red	349	46	0212
⊔	Light red	350	11	0213
⊘	Flame	608	330	0207
—	Peach	3340	328	0301
→	Dull red	347	13	0407
←	Dark orange	900	333	0208
H	Deep orange	946	332	0206
⊹	Bright orange	947	329	0205
✳	Dark green	935	862	1505
5	Green	580	267	1608
6	Yellowish green	581	266	1609
÷	Bright green	907	255	1410
K	Light green	472	264	1414
+	Dull orange	721	324	0308
△	Grey	646	273	1812
↑	Dark red	498	19	0511
⊓	Bright red	606	335	0209
	Black*	310	403	Black

Note: Backstitch flower centres in black* (used for backstitch only), fringe
on red flowers in dark red, fringe on yellow flowers in bright yellow,
tendrils in either yellowish green or green (consult the photograph), basket
in dark grey, fringe on orange flowers in dark orange, and fringe on
salmon-coloured flowers in bright red.

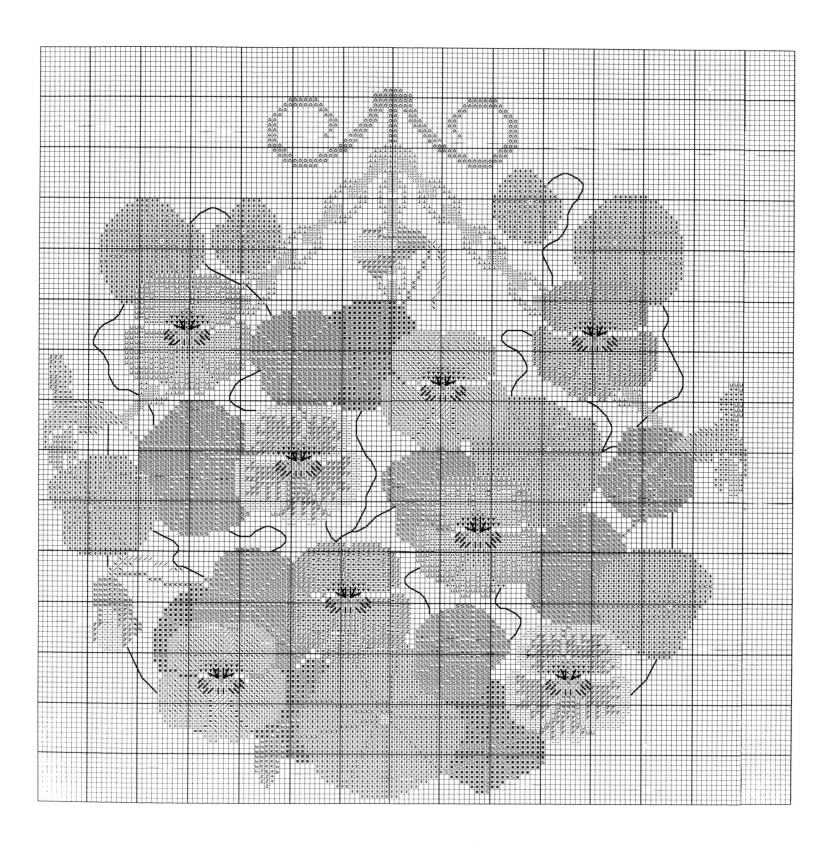

Baskets and Wreaths

A profusion of white lace and flowers gives a light and airy feel to these cushions. The bright shades of the roses are complemented by the gentler blue and mauve flowers, making this trio a delightful addition to any home.

BASKETS AND WREATHS

YOU WILL NEED

For each Cushion, measuring 40cm (16in) square:

21.5cm (8½in) square of Zweigart's white, 14-count Aida fabric
Stranded embroidery cotton in the colours given in the panel
No24 tapestry needle
42cm (16½in) square of lace fabric
Two 42cm (16½in) squares of white backing fabric
85cm (34in) of gathered lace edging, 5cm (2in) wide, for the edge of the embroidered panel
1.8m (2yds) of gathered lace edging, 4cm (1½in) wide, for the edge of the cushion
42.5cm (17in) square cushion pad

Note: To make the easy care cover, you will need, in place of the two squares of backing fabric, one 42cm (16½in) square and two more pieces, both 42cm (16½in) long, one 23cm (9in) wide, and one 33cm (13in) wide

•

THE EMBROIDERY

Prepare the fabric and stretch it in a frame (see *Basic Skills* pages 8–11). Following the chart, start the embroidery at the centre of the design, using two strands of embroidery cotton in the needle. Work each stitch over a block of fabric in each direction, making sure that all the top crosses run in the same direction and each row is worked into the same holes as the top or bottom of the row before, so that you do not leave a space between the rows.

MAKING UP

Each cover is made up in the same way. Gently steam press the embroidered fabric on the reverse side, then turn under 12mm (½in) on all sides, mitring the corners (see *Basic Skills* pages 8–11). Baste the wider lace edging around the embroidered fabric, just under the turned edge and join the ends of the lace with a narrow French seam.

Centre the panel over the lace fabric. Pin it in position and then appliqué the panel to the lace by slipstitching around the edge through all layers.

Take the remaining lace edging and, again joining the ends with a narrow French seam, pin and baste it around the edge of the lace fabric. The decorative edge should face inward and the straight edge of the lace should lie parallel to the edge of the fabric and just inside the 12mm (½in) seam allowance.

Take one of the pieces of backing fabric and lay the prepared lace fabric over it, still with the frill lying flat on the lace, facing inward. With the wrong side of the lace fabric to the right side of the backing, pin, baste and stitch through all three layers, stitching through the straight edge of the lace, just within the 12mm (½in) seam allowance.

With right sides together, join the remaining piece of backing fabric to the cushion front, leaving a 25cm (10in) gap at one side. Turn the cover right side out; insert the pad, and slipstitch to close.

EASY CARE VERSION

If you prefer a cover that can quickly be slipped off and on, for ease of laundering, you can make one with an overlap across the centre back.

Make up the front of the cover as described above. Take the wider of the two pieces of backing fabric; neaten one of the long edges and then press and stitch a 12mm (½in) hem. Take the other piece, and again on a long edge turn under 6mm (¼in) and then a further 12mm (½in) and hem. Lay the shorter piece over the longer one, overlapping the prepared edges, to make a 42cm (16½in) square; baste and stitch the sides.

Place the prepared back and cushion front with right sides together and, taking a 12mm (½in) seam, stitch all around the edge. Turn the cover right side out and insert the cushion pad through the opening across the back.

▶ BASKETS AND WREATHS		DMC	ANCHOR	MADEIRA
<	Light pink	776	73	0606
+	Medium pink	894	26	0408
O	Dark pink	892	28	0413
@	Mauve	208	111	0804
V	Yellow	745	292	0112
%	Light blue	932	920	1602
—	Dark blue	930	922	1005
S	Light green	369	213	1309
=	Medium green	368	214	1310
‡	Dark green	367	216	1312
X	Light brown	950	882	2309
>	Dark brown	407	914	2312

52

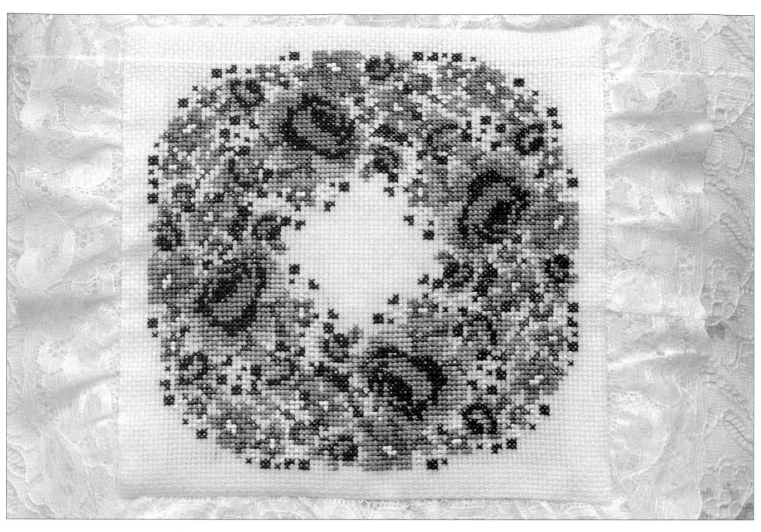

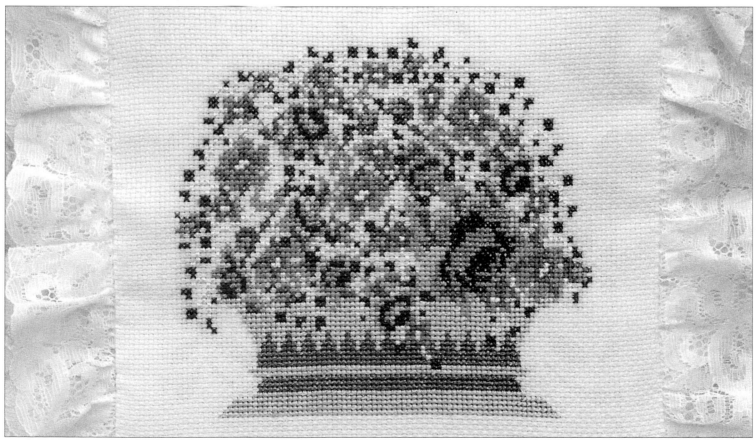

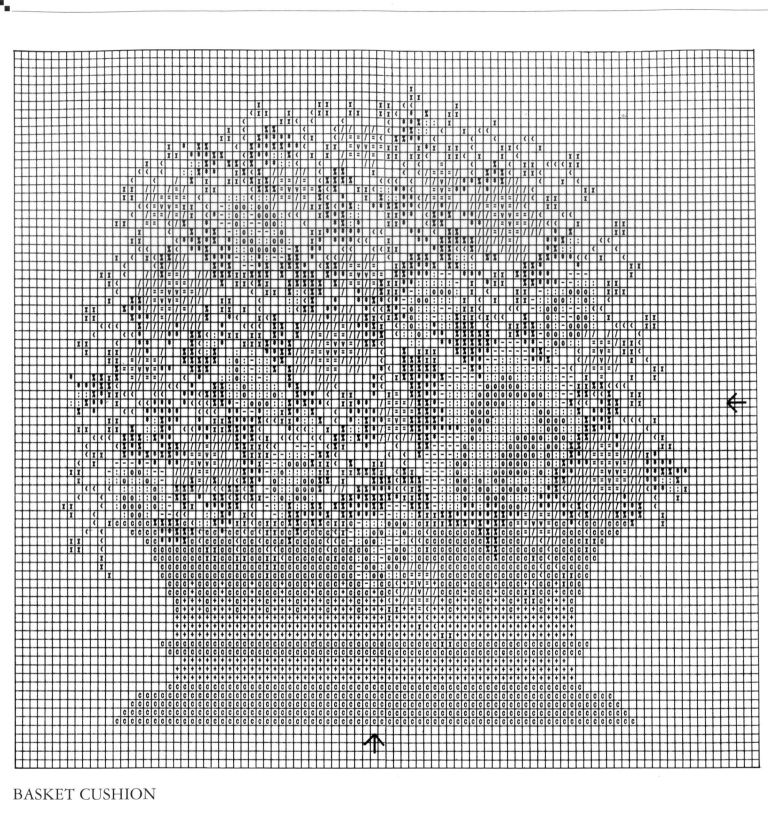

BASKET CUSHION

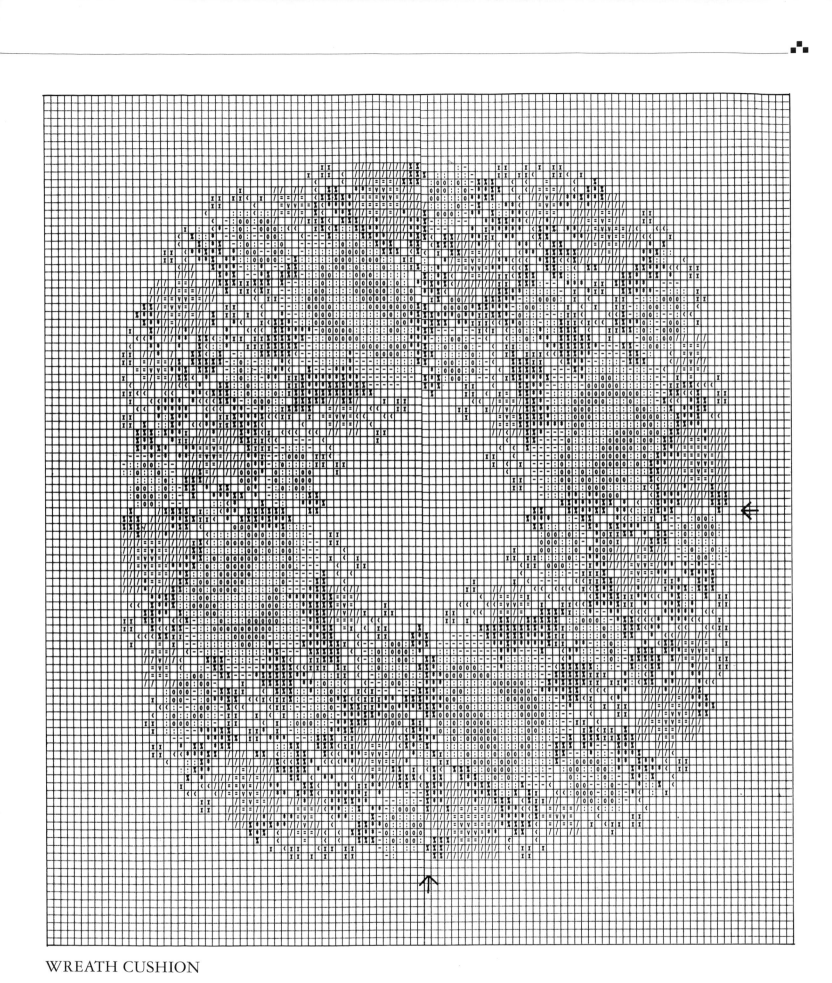

WREATH CUSHION

Tiffany Iris Cushion

Louis Comfort Tiffany used the wealth of his family jewellery firm to pioneer new methods of producing glass. Famous for his lamps, many patrons commissioned him to design windows. Here, the black fabric sets off the glowing colours of his iris.

Sunflower
Cushion

Stitch this colourful cushion and
capture the warmth of long summer
days. This project would be guaranteed
to brighten any corner of your home,
but it would also make a practical and
very unusual golden wedding present.

Nightdress Case

Sleep-inducing poppies have been chosen to decorate this pretty nightdress case – not the usual red ones, but the soft and delicate blues of the Himalayan poppy, *Meconopsis grandis*.

NIGHTDRESS CASE

YOU WILL NEED

For the Nightdress Case, measuring 35cm (1¾in) square (exclusive of broderie anglaise), with art inset for embroidery of cream, 18-count Aida fabric, measuring 18cm (7in) square:

Stranded embroidery cotton in the colours given in the panel
No26 tapestry needle
Nightdress or cushion case, available from needlework shops

●

THE EMBROIDERY

Find the centre point on your square of Aida and, beginning at the centre of the pattern, embroider the blue poppy motif, using two strands of cotton in the needle for the cross stitch and one strand of cotton for the backstitch. Steam press on the reverse side.

TO COMPLETE THE CASE

Handstitch the remaining three sides of the inset embroidered panel into place.

▶ MECONOPSIS		DMC	ANCHOR	MADEIRA
·	Cream	746	275	0101
□	Grey blue	931	921	1711
△	Deep turquoise	518	168	1106
○	Turquoise	519	167	1105
⊠	Pale blue	775	128	1001
∧	Blue	334	145	1003
—	Pink	3689	49	0607
H	Orange	721	324	0308
·ǀ·	Light orange	722	323	0307
ᑲ	Green	3053	859	1510
■	Dark green	3051	861	1508
▣	Mid green	3052	860	1509
÷	Pale green	3348	265	1409
◸	Yellowish green	472	264	1414
+	Yellowish brown	676	891	2208
◹	Pale yellow	745	300	0111
	Black*	310	403	Black

Note: Backstitch the centre and back of the flowers in black.

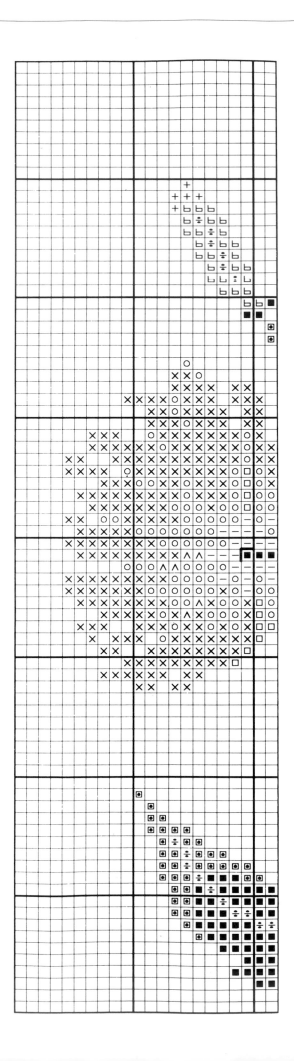

Daffodil Wreath Cushion

The cheerful yellow of the daffodils shines out brightly from the black background of this cushion, bringing a breath of spring into your home on even the darkest days.

Red Rose Cushion

The bold use of colour in this design of red roses on a navy blue background brings a traditional Berlin woolwork design right up to date, while still retaining the quality and feel of the original woolwork embroidery.

Floral Greetings

Elegant notelets, pretty gift tags and romantic designs for heartfelt messages — these beautiful little designs can be stitched in very little time and will serve as a lasting reminder of your good wishes.

ROSES WITH LOVE

YOU WILL NEED

For either the Rosy Posy Card or the Wild Rose
Card, each measuring 15cm x 20.5cm (6in x 8in)
overall, with a portrait cut-out measuring
11cm x 15cm (4½in x 6in):

*15cm x 19cm (6in x 7½in) of 'Zweigart's cream,
18-count Aida fabric
Stranded embroidery cotton in the colours given in the
appropriate panel
No24 tapestry needle
Card mount, landscape or portrait, as required*

For the Rose Garland Card, measuring 15.5cm x
11cm (6¼in x 4½in), with a cut-out measuring
8cm (3in) in diameter:

*10cm (4in) square of Zweigart's cream, 18-count
Aida fabric
Stranded embroidery cotton in the colours given in the
appropriate panel
No24 tapestry needle*

●

THE EMBROIDERY

Prepare the fabric for your chosen card and stretch
it in a frame (see *Basic Skills* pages 8–11).
Following the appropriate chart, start the embroidery at the centre of the design, using one strand of
embroidery cotton in the needle. Work each stitch
over one block of fabric in each direction. Make
sure that all the top crosses go in the same direction and that each row is worked into the same
holes as the top or bottom of the row before, so that
you do not leave a space between the rows.

MAKING UP THE CARDS

Trim the embroidery to about 12mm (½in) larger
than the cut-out window. Open out the self-adhesive mount and centre your embroidery behind the
aperture. Fold the card and press firmly to secure.
Some cards require a dab of glue for a secure and
neat finish.

▶ WILD ROSE		DMC	ANCHOR	MADEIRA
❘	Light pink	818	48	0502
△	Medium pink	776	73	0606
▬	Dark pink	899	40	0609
⊥	Light yellow	3078	292	0102
✛	Medium yellow	743	301	0113
÷	Light green	3348	264	1409
⊞	Medium green	3347	266	1408
◆	Dark green	3345	268	1406
⊡	Light brown	434	365	2009
●	Medium brown	829	906	2106

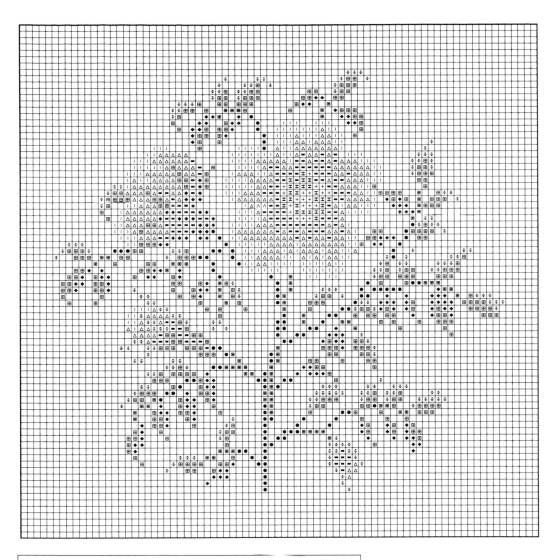

◄ ROSY POSY

		DMC	ANCHOR	MADEIRA
−	Light pink	894	26	0408
∧	Medium pink	892	28	0413
⊟	Dark pink	304	47	0511
△	Light green	3348	264	1409
⊡	Medium green	3052	844	1509
▼	Dark green	3051	845	1508

► ROSE GARLAND

		DMC	ANCHOR	MADEIRA
6	Light pink	776	73	0606
⋉	Medium pink	899	40	0609
▲	Dark pink	309	42	0510
⊥	Light peach	948	778	0306
⊞	Medium peach	353	6	0304
◪	Dark peach	754	868	0305
⊠	Yellow	743	301	0113
⊡	Light blue	932	920	1602
▬	Medium blue	931	921	1003
▼	Dark blue	930	922	1005
▷	Light green	3348	264	1409
M	Medium green	470	266	1502
▼	Dark green	936	263	1507

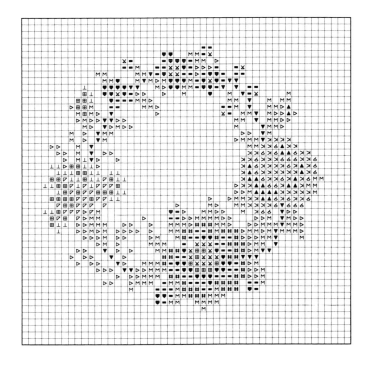

Floral Bouquet Cards

Equally suitable for a birthday, to wish a friend the best of luck, or to offer congratulations or thanks, these pretty cards are quick and easy to stitch.

FLORAL BOUQUET CARDS

YOU WILL NEED

For each Card, with an oval aperture measuring
8.5cm x 6cm (3½in x 2½in):

15cm (6in) square of white, 14-count Aida fabric
Stranded embroidery cotton in the colours given in the
appropriate panel
No26 tapestry needle
15cm (6in) of ribbon, 4mm wide
Card as specified above (for suppliers, see page 256)

Note: One skein of each colour on the combined list is
sufficient for all four designs

●

THE EMBROIDERY

Prepare the fabric (see *Basic Skills* pages 8–11); find
the centre either by folding the fabric in half and
then in half again, and lightly pressing the folded
corner, or by marking the horizontal and vertical
centre lines with basting stitches in a light-
coloured thread. Mount the fabric in a small hoop.

Following the chart, complete all the cross
stitching first, using two strands of thread in the
needle. Be careful not to take dark threads across
the back of the work in such a way that they show
through on the right side.

FINISHING

Remove the basting stitches (if any) and lightly
press. Tie the ribbon in a small bow and secure it
to the embroidery with a couple of neat stitches.

Trim the embroidery to measure 12mm (½in)
larger all around than the size of the card window.
Position the embroidery behind the window; open
out the self-adhesive mount; fold the card, and
press firmly to secure it. Some cards require a dab
of glue to ensure a secure and neat finish.

▼ PANSIES		ANCHOR	DMC	MADEIRA
::	Gold	306	725	0114
☐	Orange	324	721	0309
◯	Light green	239	702	1306
●	Medium green	210	561	1312
X	Blue	145	799	0910
+	Lilac	109	209	0803
■	Purple	102	550	0714

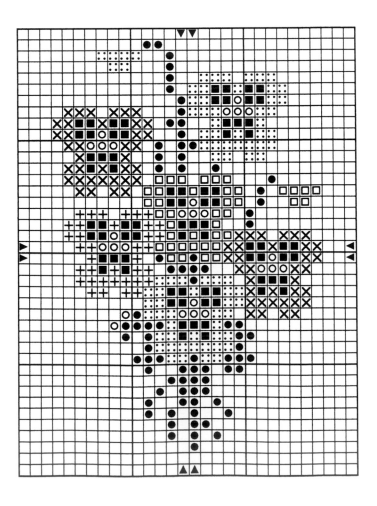

COMPLETE THREAD LIST		ANCHOR	DMC	MADEIRA
::	Gold	306	725	0114
☐	Orange	324	721	0309
·	Pink	38	335	0610
▬	Red	59	600	0704
◯	Light green	239	702	1306
●	Medium green	210	561	1312
X	Blue	145	799	0910
+	Lilac	109	209	0803
■	Purple	102	550	0714

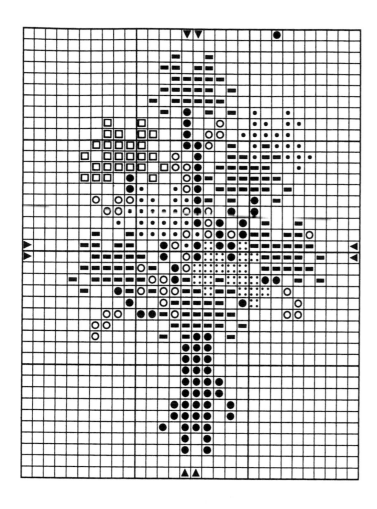

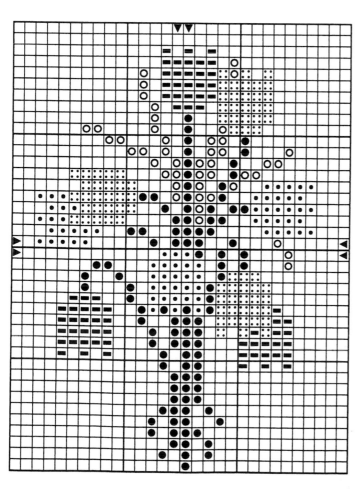

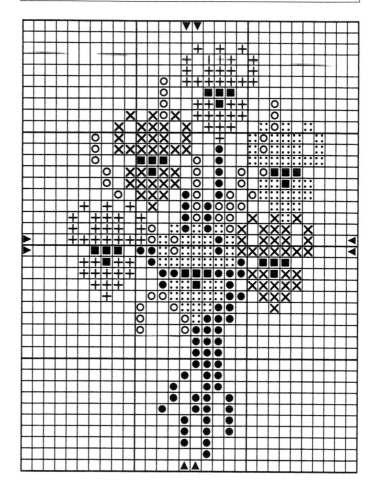

◀ DAHLIAS		ANCHOR	DMC	MADEIRA
::	Gold	306	725	0114
□	Orange	324	721	0309
•	Pink	38	335	0610
▬	Red	59	600	0704
○	Light green	239	702	1306
●	Medium green	210	561	1312

▲ IRISES		ANCHOR	DMC	MADEIRA
::	Gold	306	725	0114
○	Light green	239	702	1306
●	Medium green	210	561	1312
X	Blue	145	799	0910
+	Lilac	109	209	0803
■	Purple	102	550	0714

◀ TULIPS		ANCHOR	DMC	MADEIRA
::	Gold	306	725	0114
•	Pink	38	335	0610
▬	Red	59	600	0704
○	Light green	239	702	1306
●	Medium green	210	561	1312

Assisi Stationery

The background is stitched and the motifs left open in Assisi work. Here, this traditional style is used to feature a sprig of mint, a snip of chervil and a chicory flower. The background can easily shrink or expand to fit different objects.

ASSISI STATIONERY

YOU WILL NEED

For the Mint Trinket Box, with an oval lid measuring 5cm x 7.3cm (2in x 2⅞in):

10cm x 12cm (4in x 4¾in) of 16-count, cream Aida fabric
Stranded embroidery cotton as given in the appropriate panel
No24 tapestry needle
Trinket box (for suppliers, see page 256)

For the Mint Greeting Card, with an aperture measuring 9cm x 6cm (3½in x 2½in):

11.5cm x 8½cm (4½in x 3½in) of 14-count, cream Aida fabric
Stranded embroidery cotton and needle, as above
Greetings card (for suppliers, see page 256)

For the Chicory Flower Greetings Card, with an aperture measuring 6cm (2½in) square

8.5cm (3½in) square of 14-count, white Aida fabric
Standard embroidery cotton and needle, as above
Greetings card (for suppliers, see page 256)

For the Chervil Paperweight, measuring 7cm (2¾in) in diameter:

10cm (4in) square of 14-count, white Aida fabric
Standard embroidery cotton and needle, as above
Paperweight (for suppliers, see page 256)

THE EMBROIDERY

For each design, mark the centre of the fabric both ways with lines of basting stitches (see *Basic Skills* pages 8–11) and either work with the fabric held in the hand or in a small hoop (see *Basic Skills* pages 8–11). Using one strand of embroidery cotton in the needle for the mint design, and two strands for the chicory or chervil designs, complete all the backstitching. Using two strands of embroidery cotton in the needle for all designs, cross stitch around the outer boundary of the design, and then fill in the gap between the outer line and the inner line of backstitching that outlines the motif.

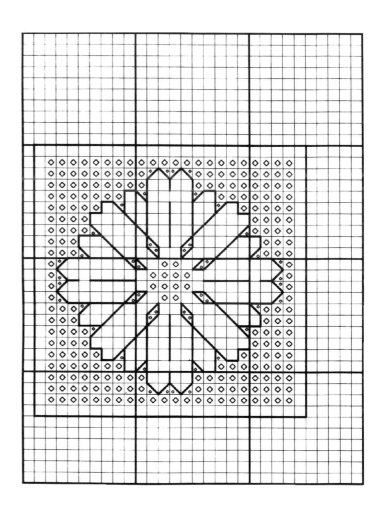

▲ ASSISI STATIONERY			
Mint	DMC	ANCHOR	MADEIRA
● Green	3345	263	1507
Chervil			
▲ Purple	327	112	0713
Chicory			
◇ Light brown	435	308	2212

GREETINGS CARDS

Trim the embroidered fabric to fit the inside of the card and remove the basting stitches. Position the embroidery centrally behind the cut-out, then fold over the front flap of the card and press (you may need to add a small piece of double-sided tape to secure it).

TRINKET BOX AND PAPERWEIGHT

Mark both ways across the centre of the template provided. Lay the embroidery face down on a clean surface and centre the template over it, matching the pencil lines and the basted centre lines. Lightly draw around the outline and then cut the fabric to shape. Remove the basting stitches and complete the assembly, following the manufacturer's instructions.

Wedding Celebrations

Your guests will be delighted with this wedding place card and almond bag as souvenirs, while the gift tag and wedding card will show that you have put a little extra thought into your wedding present.

Sophie

Art Nouveau Florals

These simple designs use only whole stitches, making them quick to sew. The flowing lines of the iris and poppy are complemented by the linear style of the lily and begonia. Look for special trimmings or frames to show off your projects.

Boudoir Trinkets

Pretty feminine items like the pansy spray box with a touch of sparkle or the lavender drawer scenter make beautiful gifts — or why not spoil yourself and keep some for your own "boudoir"?

ROSE JEWELLERY BOX

YOU WILL NEED

For the Jewellery Box measuring approximately 19 cm (7½in) square and 8cm (3¼in) high:

*25cm (10in) square of white, 14-count
Aida fabric
Stranded embroidery cotton in the colours listed
in the panel
No26 tapestry needle
50cm (18in) of cotton fabric for the box cover, cut as
follows: four 21.5cm (8½in) squares and four pieces
21.5cm x 17.5cm (8½in x 7in)
Lightweight wadding (batting): one piece 19cm (7½in)
square and four pieces 19cm x 7.5cm (7½in x 3in)
Medium-weight card: three 19cm (7½in) squares,
one of them with a 15cm (6in) circular aperture,
one 18cm (7in) square,
and four pieces 19cm x 7.5cm (7½in x 3in)
Lightweight card: one 16cm (6½in) square
38cm (15in) of medium-weight piping cord
Matching sewing cotton
5cm (2in) of ribbon, 12mm (½in) wide
Glue stick
Masking tape*

•

THE EMBROIDERY

Prepare the fabric (see *Basic Skills* pages 8–11); find the centre either by folding the fabric in half and then in half again, and lightly pressing the folded corner, or by marking the horizontal and vertical centre lines with basting stitches in a light-coloured thread. Mount the fabric in a frame (see *Basic Skills* pages 8–11) and work out from the centre.

Following the chart, complete all the cross stitching first, using two strands of thread in the needle. Finish with the backstitching, using one strand of thread in the needle. Be careful not to take dark threads across the back of the embroidery in such a way that they show through on the right side.

Remove the finished embroidery from the hoop or frame and wash it if necessary, then press lightly on the reverse side, using a steam iron.

THE BOX

To prepare the side sections, first glue a piece of wadding to one side of each of the four 19cm x 7.5cm (7½in x 3in) pieces of card. For each side, take a piece of cotton fabric 21.5cm x 17.5cm (8½in x 7in) and lay a card, padded side down, on the wrong side of the fabric, with an allowance of 12mm (½in) of fabric showing at each side and the bottom edge. Fold the sides and tape them; bring the upper section of fabric over the card and turn the raw edge under stitch along the lower edge, so that the stitching line is just slightly to the back of the card (not along the bottom). Oversewing the edges with neat stitches, join the sides of the box together to make a square, with the padded sides facing out and the stitched lower edges facing in.

Take two of the square cards (for the base) and cover one side of each with a piece of fabric. Fold in the sides, mitring the corners. and secure with tape (see *Basic Skills* pages 8–11). Push one piece, fabric side down, into the base of the box, and neatly oversew the base to the bottom edges. Turn the box over and neatly stitch the cord along the top edge of one side (now the back edge), allowing the ends to run down the inside corners and on to the base. Push the second base piece, fabric side up, into the box, covering the cord ends and the back of the first base section.

Cover the 18cm (7½in) card (inside lid), using the same method as for the base card. Glue the remaining piece of wadding to the card with the aperture and cut around the edge of the circle to remove the wadding from the centre. Do this carefully, because this piece of wadding is then glued to the centre of the lightweight card.

	▶ ROSE JEWELLERY BOX	ANCHOR	DMC	MADEIRA
·	White	1	White	White
O	Yellow	305	726	0112
●	Deep yellow	306	725	0113
∷	Pale pink	73	3689	0607
X	Light plum	76	3731	0610
□	Medium plum	65	816	0704
■	Dark plum	45	814	0513
—	Pale green	254	472	1409
V	Light green	256	906	1411
◇	Medium green	258	904	1413
◆	Dark green	246	319	1406

Note: Outline the leaves and stems in dark green and the flowers in dark plum, using one strand of thread in the needle.

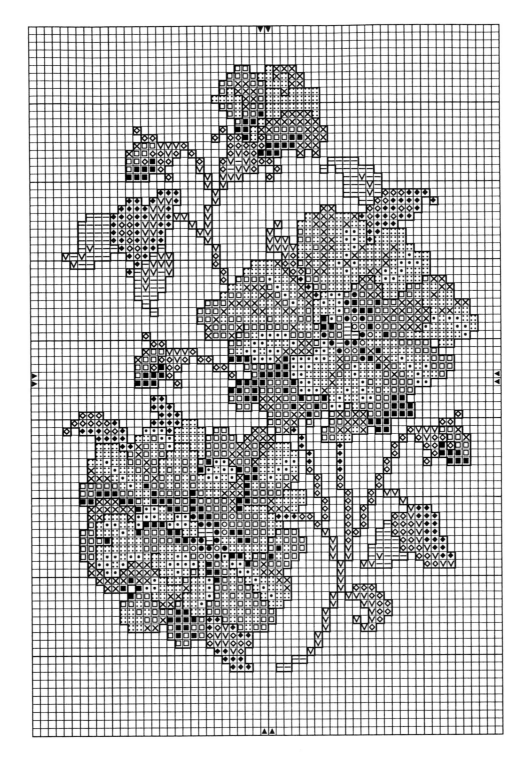

Place the card with the aperture on the final piece of fabric and fold in the sides; mitre the corners, and secure with glue.

When the glue has dried, cut out the centre, leaving an allowance of approximately 12mm (½in) of fabric for the turning. Snip into the fabric allowance at intervals of 12mm (½in); turn the fabric back over the card, and secure at the back with masking tape.

Next, place the embroidery so that the design is positioned exactly over the circular piece of wadding that you have already glued to the light-weight card. Lace the embroidery over the back of the card (see *Basic Skills* pages 8–11).

To assemble the lid, centre the mount over the embroidery, then place the inside lid at the back, forming a sandwich with the embroidery in the middle. The mount should overlap the inside lid by a margin of about 6mm (¼in). Insert the ribbon, folded in half, between the inside lid and the mount to make the front opening tag. Neatly stitch the inside lid to the mounted embroidery. Finally, oversew the back of the lid to the cord at the back edge of the box.

Miniature Studies

These exquisite miniatures in their elaborate frames and jewellery bases would complement any outfit. Memories of great-grandmothers wearing high-necked dresses and beautiful jewellery, are reflected in these designs.

MINIATURE STUDIES

YOU WILL NEED

For the Wreath Brooch, with a design size measuring 4cm (1½in) in diameter:

8cm (3¼in) square of antique white, 28-count evenweave linen
Stranded embroidery cotton in the colours given in the appropriate panel
No24 tapestry needle
Miniature jewellery frame for mounting the embroidery (for suppliers, see page 256)

For the Bouquet Brooch, with a design size measuring 4cm x 3cm (1½in x 1¼in):

8cm x 7cm (3¼in x 2¾in) of antique white, 28-count evenweave linen
Stranded embroidery cotton in the colours given in the appropriate panel
No24 tapestry needle
Miniature jewellery frame for mounting the embroidery (for suppliers, see page 256)

For the Rose Picture, with a design size measuring 4cm x 3cm (1½in x 1¼in):

8cm x 7cm (3¼in x 2¾in) of antique white, 28-count evenweave linen
Stranded embroidery cotton in the colours given in the appropriate panel
No24 tapestry needle
Miniature jewellery frame for mounting the embroidery (for suppliers, see page 256)

THE EMBROIDERY

Mark the centre of each piece of fabric with a vertical and horizontal line of basting stitches. As the fabric is so small, it is not necessary to mount it in a frame; instead it can be worked in the hand.

Starting at the centre of the design, and using one strand of embroidery thread in the needle, work each cross stitch over one thread of fabric in each direction, following the chart. Work the backstitch on the Bouquet Brooch design with one strand of thread, as indicated in the key.

FINISHING

Steam press the completed embroidery gently on the reverse side, then mount the embroidery in the jewellery frame as explained in the manufacturer's instructions.

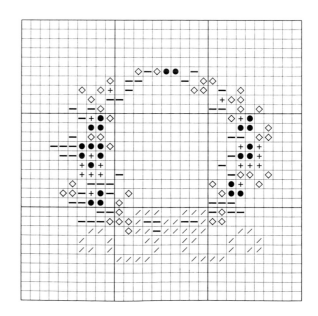

▲ WREATH		DMC	ANCHOR	MADEIRA
∕	Mauve	208	111	0712
●	Light pink	776	73	0606
+	Dark pink	899	40	0609
▬	Dark green	3347	266	1408
◇	Light green	3348	264	1501

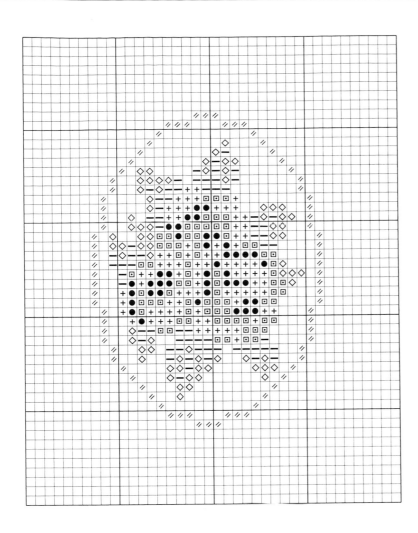

◄ ROSE PICTURE		DMC	ANCHOR	MADEIRA
●	Dark red	304	47	0511
⁄	Grey	415	398	1803
+	Light red	666	46	0510
⊡	Pink	892	28	0411
▬	Dark green	3347	266	1408
◇	Light green	3348	264	1501

► BOUQUET		DMC	ANCHOR	MADEIRA
⊡	Light pink	776	73	0606
⁄	Blue	798	131	0911
+	Pink	899	40	0609
▬	Dark green	3347	266	1408
◇	Light green	3348	264	1501
●	Dark pink	3350	65	0603

Note: Backstitch stems in dark green.

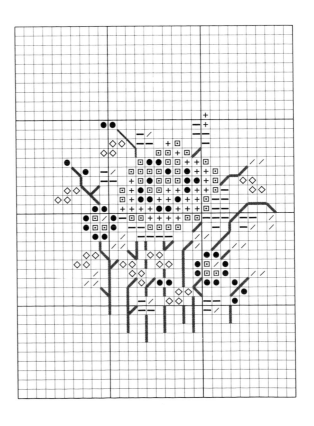

Tiffany
Treasures

Stitch a tiny treasure for a special friend. The dragonfly, based on a stained glass suncatcher, fits on to a spectacles case. A fragment of Tiffany's 'Dogwood' design adorns a powder compact, and a miniature lamp decorates a trinket box lid.

TIFFANY TREASURES

YOU WILL NEED

For the Spectacles Case, with a design area measuring 7.5cm x 5cm (3in x 2in):

Ready-made black quilted spectacles case with 18-count Aida fabric insert (for suppliers, see page 256)
Stranded embroidery cotton and specialist thread in the colours listed in the appropriate panel
No26 tapestry needle

For the Powder Compact, with a design area measuring 6.5cm (2½in) in diameter:

15cm (6in) square of black, 28-count evenweave fabric
Stranded embroidery cotton in the colours listed in the appropriate panel
No26 tapestry needle
Powder compact (for suppliers, see page 256)

For the Trinket Box, with a design area measuring 7.5cm x 5cm (3in x 2in):

15cm (6in) square of black, 28-count evenweave fabric
Stranded embroidery cotton and specialist thread in the colours listed in the appropriate panel
No26 tapestry needle
Trinket box (for suppliers, see page 256)

●

THE SPECTACLES CASE

Find the centre of Aida fabric flap on the case (the most accurate way to do this is count the number of squares in each direction). Then refer to *Basic Skills* (pages 8–11) for working with specialist threads.

Using one strand of stranded cotton or rayon thread, complete all the cross stitching following the chart. Work the backstitch using two strands of thread in the needle. Lightly press the flap on the reverse side.

THE POWDER COMPACT

Prepare the fabric and find the centre point (see *Basic Skills* pages 8–11). Using two strands of thread in the needle and stitching over two threads of fabric, complete all the cross stitching following the chart. Work the backstitching using one strand of thread in the needle.

Assemble the compact according to the manufacturer's instructions. (Note that the design will go right to the edges of the compact lid with no fabric showing.)

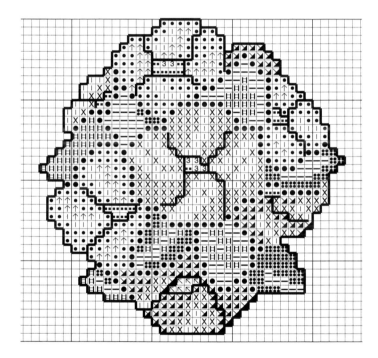

▲ DOGWOOD COMPACT		DMC	ANCHOR	MADEIRA
·	White	01	02	2402
▬	Green	470	268	1503
⊟	Medium green	471	266	1501
3	Yellow	727	293	0110
↖	Tangerine	742	303	0114
❚❚	Gold	783	307	2211
❙	Light pink	818	230	502
	Dark brown*	838	380	2005
●	Dark grey	844	1041	1810
⦂⦂	Dark gren	937	269	1504
⊠	Dark pink	961	76	0610
⊠	Medium pink	962	75	0609
↑	Cream	3823	386	251

Note: Backstatch outlines using dark brown (*used for backstitch only).*

122

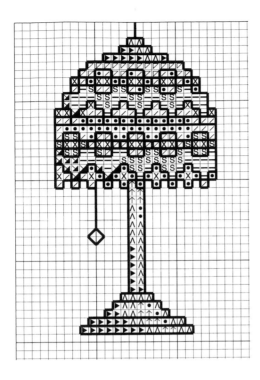

◀ LAMP TRINKET BOX	DMC	ANCHOR	MADEIRA	MARLITT/ KREINIK
Black*	310	403	Black	–
⊠ Dark purple x 2 plus purple rayon x 1	550	101	0714	819
▬ Purple x 2 plus medium purple rayon x 1	552	99	0713	858
· White	01	02	2402	–
▧ Light purple	211	342	0801	–
S Medium purple	554	96	0711	–
∧ Yellow	725	305	0108	–
↑ Light yellow	727	293	0110	–
X Tangerine	742	303	0114	–
▶ Gold	783	307	2211	–
◪ Cream	3823	386	2511	–
Bright yellow*	–	–	–	Kreinik No.8 Braid 091

Note: Backstitch switch cord and metal spike on top of lamp with Kreinik Bright Yellow; backstitch the rest of the outlines in one strand of black* (*used for backstitch only).*

THE TRINKET BOX

Prepare the fabric and find the centre point (see *Basic Skills* pages 8–11). Some areas of the design require stranded cotton and rayon blending filament to be blended. Using two strands of cotton and one of rayon, follow the instructions in *Basic Skills* (pages 8–11) for working with specialist threads. Complete the backstitch details, following the key. Assemble the box lid according to the manufacturer's instructions.

▼ DRAGONFLY CASE	DMC	ANCHOR	MADEIRA	MARLITT
· White	01	02	2402	–
Black*	310	403	Black	–
● Orange	608	332	0205	–
← Tangerine	742	303	0114	–
◇ Yellow	744	301	0112	–
◤ Aqua	–	–	–	1053
⦂⦂ Dark aqua	–	–	–	1056
X Light blue	3811	928	1111	–
‖ Cream	3823	386	2511	–

Note: Backstitch outlines using two strands of black (*used for backstitch only).*

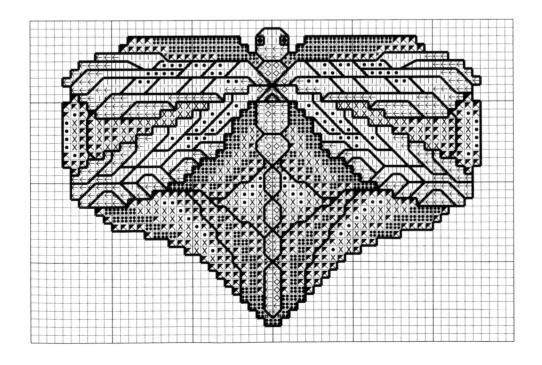

Pansy Spray Box

This richly embellished fan-shaped box, decorated with sparkling metallic threads and beads, would make a pretty gift for a special friend, or a future heirloom in which to store jewellery and other keepsakes.

PANSY SPRAY BOX

YOU WILL NEED

For the Pansy Box, with a design size measuring
15cm x 9cm (6in x 3½in):

*22.5cm x 18cm (9in x 7¼in) of antique white,
14-count Aida fabric
Stranded cotton and specialist thread in the colours
given in the panel
No24 tapestry needle
Seed beads in the colours given
in the panel
Beading needle
Fan box kit (for supplier see page 256)
22.5cm x 18cm (9in x 7¼in) of wadding
25cm (10in) square of pink felt
Fabric glue*

●

THE EMBROIDERY

Prepare the fabric and mount it in a frame (see *Basic Skills* pages 8–11). Then mark the central horizontal and vertical lines on the fabric using basting stitches.

Following the chart, start the embroidery in the centre of the design, using two strands of embroidery thread in the needle. Embroider the areas of stranded cotton first, working each cross stitch over one block of fabric in each direction. Then embroider the areas of metallic thread, using two strands of thread as before (see *Basic Skills* pages 8–11 for tips on working with metallic thread).

Work the backstitch using two strands of metallic cotton. Sew the pink and gold beads in place (see *Basic Skills* pages 8–11).

FINISHING

Remove the embroidery from the frame and place it face down on a thick towel. Then gently steam press it. Cover the box with wadding and pink felt, securing it with fabric glue, then assemble the box as explained in the manufacturer's instructions.

▶ PANSY SPRAY	DMC	ANCHOR	MADEIRA	KREINIK
⊞ Dark pink	815	22	0512	–
◪ Pink	3804	63	0703	–
⊘ Light pink	3806	60	0701	–
Gold blending filament*	–	–	–	002
✚ Green blending filament	–	–	–	008
▬ Dark green blending filament*	–	–	–	009
◈ Light green blending filament	–	–	–	015
· Antique gold beads V2.08.3820	–	–	–	–
S Shocking pink beads V3.01.917	–	–	–	–

Note: Backstitch fan edge and honeycomb pattern at base of fan in gold blending filament*; backstitch flower stems in dark green blending filament* (*used for backstitch only).
One spool of blending filament in each colour, and one packet of beads in each colour are required.

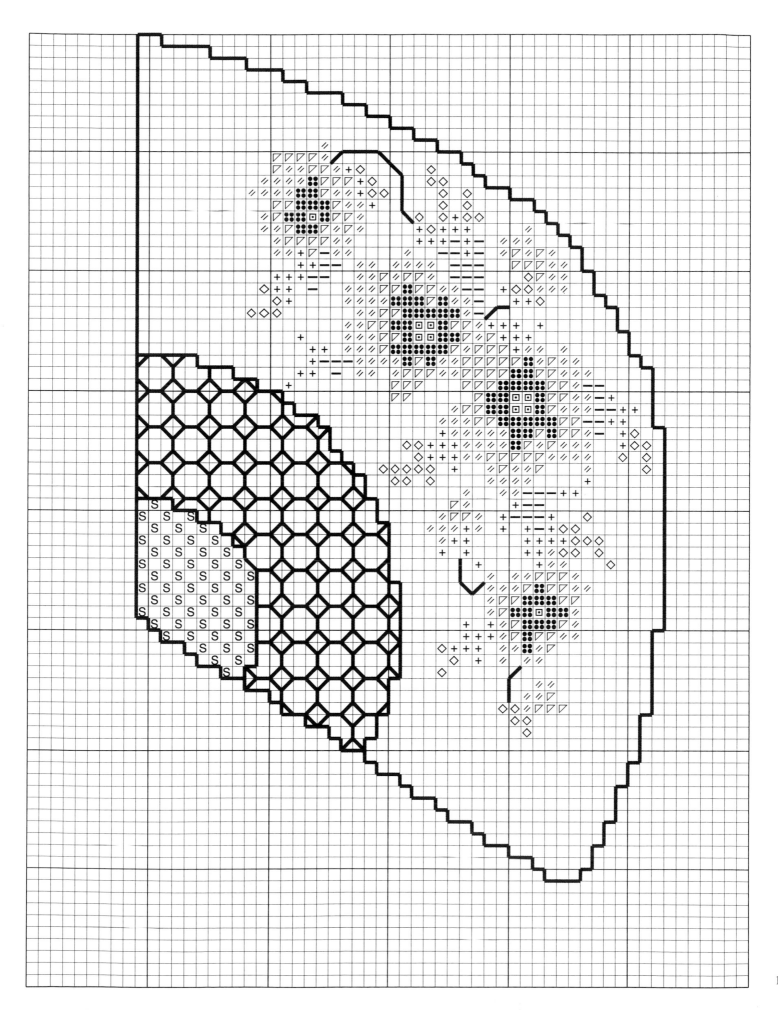

Glasgow Roses

Charles Rennie Mackintosh was one of the most influential architects of his day. Together with his wife Margaret, he created restful interiors and the rose was one of their favourite symbols. Stitch a sampler or smaller items in this style.

GLASGOW ROSES

YOU WILL NEED

For the Sampler, with a design area measuring
18.5cm x 16.5cm (7⅜in x 6½in):

*30cm x 35cm (12in x 14in) of antique white,
28-count evenweave fabric
Stranded embroidery cotton in the colours listed
in the panel
No26 tapestry needle
Firm card for backing
Frame and mount of your choice*

FOR OTHER PROJECTS:

*Antique white 18-count Aida, in size required
Stranded embroidery cotton in the colours listed
in the panel
No26 tapestry needle
Door finger plate (for suppliers, see page 256)
Trinket box (for suppliers, see page 256)
Mirror and hairbrush set (for suppliers, see page 256)*

●

THE EMBROIDERY

Prepare the fabric and find the centre point as
explained in *Basic Skills* (pages 8–11). Using two
strands of thread in the needle and stitching over
two threads of the fabric, complete all the cross
stitching following the chart. Then work the backstitching using one strand of thread in the needle.

FINISHING

Remove the embroidery from the frame and wash,
if necessary, then press lighty on the reverse side.
An excellent choice of ready-made frames and
mounts is now widely available from art and craft
stores. If you wish to carry out your own framing,
see *Basic Skills* pages 8–11 for lacing the stitched
piece securely on to the cardboard. Alternatively,
take your sampler to a professional framer who will
advise you on suitable mounts and frame finishes.

MAKING OTHER PROJECTS

Glasgow Roses is a versatile design which allows
you to create your own unique projects. Here, elements from the sampler have been made into
inserts for a door finger plate, a silver trinket box
and a beautiful mirror and hairbrush.

To extract elements from the design, make an
enlarged photocopy of the design. If you are stitching a piece to insert in a ready-made item it is
important to have an exact measurement of the
actual design space available. Choose part of the
design, for example the large central rose, and
count the number of stitches widthways and
lengthways. Divide each of these measurements by
two and this will give you their centre lines. Mark
these on your photocopy. Where the lines intersect
will be your centre point. Now decide which fabric
you wish to use. Bear in mind that if your chosen
design is too big on 14-count Aida fabric, it will
probably fit the space if stitched on a higher count.
The rose in the trinket box was stitched on
18-count Aida. A little time spent on these calcu-
lations at this stage is well worth the effort to
avoid mistakes.

Insert the stitched piece into the door finger
plate, trinket box, or hairbrush back, following the
manufacturer's instructions.

▶ GLASGOW ROSES	DMC	ANCHOR	MADEIRA
White	01	02	2402
Gold	832	907	2202
Light gold	834	874	2510
Dark brown	838	380	2005
Medium plum	3042	870	0807
Dark green	3362	263	2603
Medium green	3363	262	1602
Light green	3364	260	1603
Dark pink	3687	68	0604
Medium pink	3688	66	0605
Light pink	3689	49	0607
Dark plum	3740	873	2614
Light plum	3743	869	2611
Magenta	3803	972	2609

Note: Backstitch outlines in dark brown.

Jewellery Roll and Box

Keep your trinkets and pieces of jewellery in a romantic trinket pot and a rich and luxurious jewellery roll, both adorned with cross stitch inspired by traditional oriental designs. The heart would also be ideal for a Valentine card.

JEWELLERY ROLL AND BOX

YOU WILL NEED

For the Jewellery Roll, measuring
49cm x 17cm (9½in x 6½in)
when opened out:

*52cm x 21cm (20½in x 8¼in) of 27-count
Linda fabric, in black
Stranded embroidery cotton in the colours given in the
appropriate panel
Gold threads as given in the appropriate panel
No26 tapestry needle
52cm x 21cm (20½in x 8¼in) of 2oz wadding,
plus scraps for ring roll
Three pieces of lining fabric as follows: one piece 79cm x
21cm (31in x 8¼in), for small pockets, and one piece
8cm x 21cm (3in x 8¼in), for ring roll
Two small strips of black velcro ot two press studs
(poppers), for fastenings*

Note: There is no exact equivalent for the
variegated cotton threads in Madeira and no exact
match for the metallic threads in either Madeira
or Anchor, but you can substitute different
threads, provided you obtain an attractive effect.

For the Trinket Pot Lid, with an inset
9cm (3½in) in diameter:

*15cm (6in) square of 28-count Quaker eavenweave
fabric, in white
Stranded embroidery cotton in the colours given in the
appropriate panel
No26 tapestry needle
Burgundy trinket pot, with a lid with an inset as
specified above (for suppliers see page 256)*

●

THE EMBROIDERY

The embroidery fabric for the jewellery roll only
includes normal seam allowances, so first oversew
the edges or protect them with masking tape to
prevent fraying. Divide the prepared fabric into
four equal sections by basting three lines 13cm
(5in) apart across the width. Baste horizontal and
vertical centre lines across one of the end sections
and embroider in this section. Embroider all cross
stitches with two strands of thread and backstitch
with one strand of gold metallic thread. When
working with metallic thread, use quite short
lengths and knot the thread at the eye of the needle to prevent slipping. When stitching with the
variegated thread, select lengths of thread which
shade strongly from dark to light rather than more
evenly shaded lengths. Work each complete cross
separately rather than stitching in rows.

For the trinket pot, prepare the fabric (see *Basic
Skills* pages 8–11). Embroider all cross stitches
with two strands of thread and backstitch with one
strand of thread. When the embroidery is complete, steam press gently on the reverse side.
Assemble the trinket pot lid according to the manufacturer's instructions.

THE JEWELLERY ROLL

Hem both short ends of the largest piece of lining
fabric: turn under and press a 6mm (¼in) hem and
then turn a further 6mm (¼in), enclosing the raw
edges. Stitch the hems by hand or machine. Also
hem one 21cm (8in) edge of the piece of lining fabric measuring 14cm x 21cm (5½in x 8in).

Fold the large piece of lining fabric in half and
mark the centre line across the width with basting
stitches. With the right sides together, place the
raw 21cm (8¼in) edge of the small pocket piece
12mm (½in) from this line and stitch in place
along the centre line. Turn the pocket piece right
side up, enclosing the raw edge, and stitch down
the centre of the pocket, through both fabrics,
dividing it in two.

For the larger pockets, turn 13cm (5in) in at each
hemmed edge and baste in position (all pockets are
on the same side of the lining). On the reverse side
of the Linda fabric, draw a curve around the
embroidered edge. Place lining and main fabrics
right sides together, then place the wadding on
top. Pin, baste and machine stitch through all layers, taking a seam allowance of 12mm (½in). Stitch
smoothly around the curve and leave the opposite
end open for turning through. Trim the wadding
close to the stitching and trim the curve 12mm
(½in) from the stitching. Clip the seam allowance
around the curve and turn the roll right side out.
Press lightly around the edges; turn in seam
allowances at the open end, and slipstitch together.

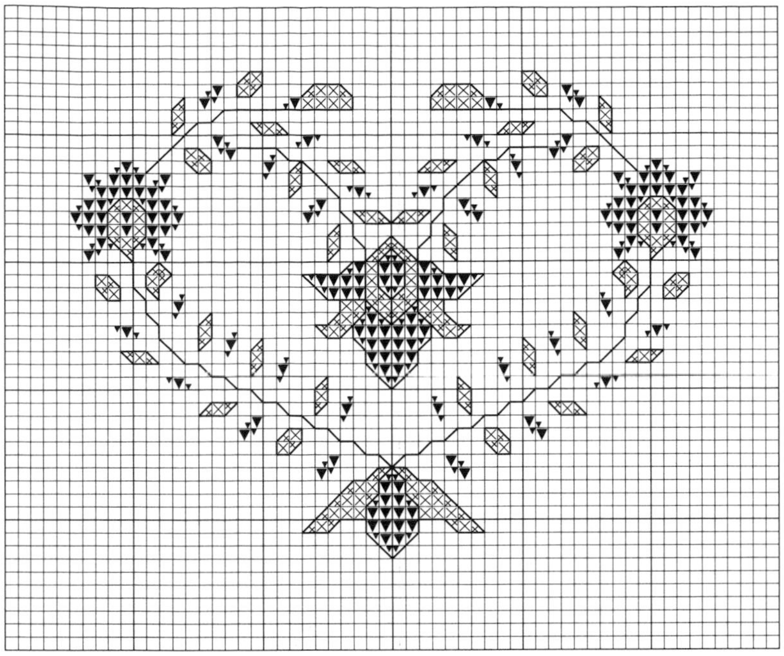

◄ ORIENTAL HEART		DMC	ANCHOR	MADEIRA
▼	Ruby red	304	19	0511
X	Pink	605	50	0612

Note: Backstitch with ruby red.

▼ ORIENTAL JEWELLERY BOX		DMC	ANCHOR
▽	Purple	95	1208
▼	Blue	113	1210
▪▪	Red	115	1206
+	Green	123	1214
↖	Gold (Or) DMC: D317 6-strand divisible metallic thread		
	Gold* DMC: Art 284 3-strand divisible metallic thread		

*Note: Backstitch with gold Art 284 (*used for backstitching only).*

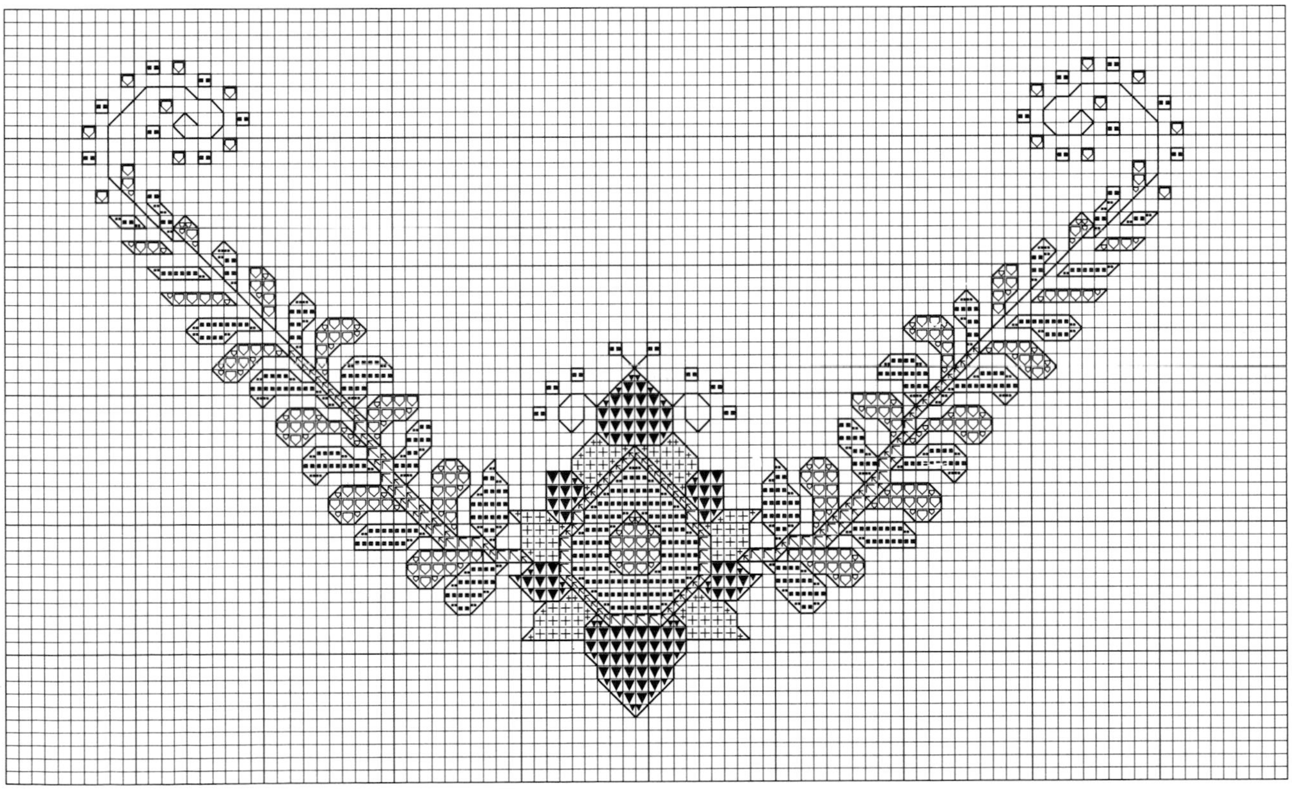

To make a small ring roll, fold the remaining strip of lining fabric in half and stitch along the long side and one short side, 12mm (½in) in from the raw edges.

Clip the corners and turn through to right side. Fill lightly with scraps of wadding then turn in the raw end and slipstitch across the opening. Place the ring roll inside the jewellery roll, in the centre of the section with no pockets; stitch one end of the ring roll a fraction from the edge of the jewellery roll. To fasten, stitch a small piece of velcro or a press stud (popper) to the other end of the ring roll and at the appropriate point on the inside of the jewellery roll.

Roll up the jewellery roll so the embroidered section sits on the top. Stitch a velcro strip or press stud on the inside, 12mm (½in) in from the centre edge of the curve, to make a sure fastening.

Romantic Keepsakes

For that christening present with a difference, here is an easy-to-make cover for an album of treasured photographs. The cover is decorated with delicate, pastel-shaded sweet peas. To complement this, why not embroider a baby's pillow with matching flowers.

ROMANTIC KEEPSAKES

YOU WILL NEED

For the cover to fit a baby's Photograph Album, measuring 21.5cm x 16cm (8½in x 6¼in):

68cm x 19cm (27in x 7½in) of cream, 18-count Aida fabric
47cm x 16.5cm (18½in x 6½in) of white interfacing
Stranded embroidery cotton in the colours given in the panel
No26 tapestry needle

For the baby's Pillow Cover, measuring 33cm (13in) square, including the broderie anglaise edging:

12.5cm (5in) square of white, 18-count Aida fabric, for the embroidered motif
32cm (12½in) square of white damask, for the front of the pillow
28cm x 32cm (11in x 12½in) and another strip 10cm x 32cm (4in x 12½in), both of white damask, for the back of the pillow
1.8m (1¾yds) of frilled insertion broderie anglaise, 5cm (2in) wide
1.8m (1¾yds) of pink or blue ribbon, of an appropriate width to slot through your broderie anglaise
Stranded embroidery cotton in the colours given in the panel
No26 tapestry needle

●

THE ALBUM COVER

Fold the Aida fabric in half, to give you a working area 34cm x 19cm (13⅓in x 7½in). With the fold on the left, measure in 19mm (¾in) from the fold and baste stitch from top to bottom. From this line, measure a further 21.5cm (8½in) across and baste another line from top to bottom. From the top edge, measure down 15mm (⅔in) and from the bottom edge measure up 15mm (⅔in). Baste along these two lines. This will leave you with a rectangular area 21.5cm x 16cm (8½in x 6¼in) for the front cover of your album. Position your embroidery centrally in this area or slightly towards the

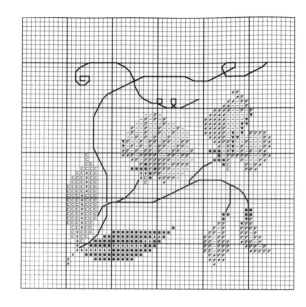

bottom left-hand corner. Use two strands of cotton for the cross stitch, two for backstitching the stalks and tendrils, and one for backstitching the fine detail on the seed pods. Gently steam press on the reverse side.

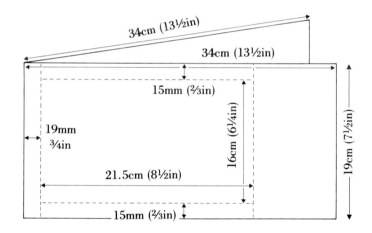

MAKING UP THE COVER

Centre the interfacing lengthwise on the Aida fabric. Fold the Aida to form a narrow hem along the edges, enclosing the interfacing. Machine stitch in position. Centre the album on the reverse side of the fabric and fold the extra width over the front and back cover. Sew a seam along the edges at the top and bottom to form a pocket at the front and back.

BABY'S PILLOW COVER

Find the centre point of the Aida and, beginning from the centre of the pattern, embroider the sweet pea motif, using two strands of cotton, both for the cross stitch and for the backstitch. Pink and blue shades are given in the key. Steam press on the reverse side.

MAKING UP THE PILLOW

Make a narrow hem on one of the 32cm (12½in) sides of the larger back piece of the damask, and repeat on one of the 32cm (12½in) sides of the narrow strip.

Cut a 9cm (3½in) square from the top left corner of the front piece of damask, and snip the inner corner of the cut area to facilitate the turning of a 6mm (¼in) hem along the two cut sides. Insert the embroidered motif and machine along the two sides.

◄ SWEET PEA PILLOW

		DMC	ANCHOR	MADEIRA
▼	Maroon	902	72	0601
∕∕	Deep pink	602	63	0702
◿	Pink	603	62	0701
—	Pale pink	605	60	0613
⊏	Dark green	3345	268	1406
⊡	Green	3346	817	1407
÷	Light green	3347	266	1408
Alternative blue shaded for boy				
▼	Dark blue	333	119	0903
∕∕	Blue	340	118	0902
◿	Light mauve	210	108	0802
—	Pale mauve	211	342	0801
⊏	Dark green	3345	268	1406
⊡	Green	3346	817	1407
÷	Light green	3347	266	1408

Note: Whether the pillow is for a boy or girl, backstitch flower stalk in green and tendrils in dark green.

▼ SWEET PEA ALBUM COVER

		DMC	ANCHOR	MADEIRA
T	Black	310	403	Black
◤	Dark blue	333	119	0903
□	Navy	939	127	1009
◇	Blue	340	118	0902
◺	Pale blue	341	117	0901
▼	Maroon	902	72	0601
∕∕	Deep pink	602	63	0702
◿	Pink	603	62	0701
—	Pale pink	605	60	0613
✳	Dark green	3345	268	1406
S	Medium green	3346	817	1407
b	Green	3347	266	1408
K	Yellowish green	472	264	1414
⊐	Purple	208	110	0804
I	Mauve	209	109	0803
△	Light mauve	210	108	0802
⊓	Pale mauve	211	342	0801
↑	Reddish purple	550	102	0714

Note: Backstitch all branches and tendrils in medium green, and the calyx of the pea pods in dark green.

With all right sides together, place the back piece of damask on the larger front piece and then the narrower strip, overlapping the two. Machine around all four sides. Turn right side out and press.

Machine the broderie anglaise into place all around the pillow on the extreme edge, mitring the corners. Slip a ready-made cot or pram pillow into the finished cover.

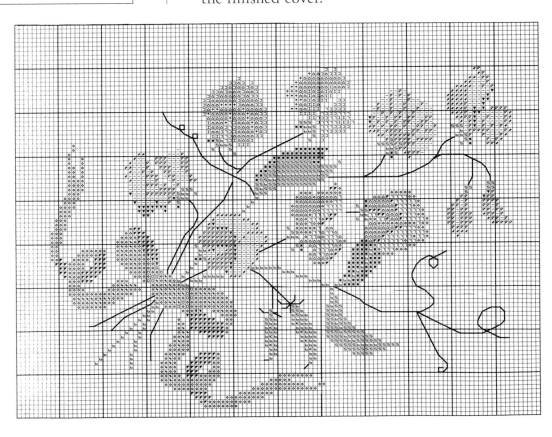

Floral Trinket Box

This fragile flower, known as Love-in-a-mist or Nigella, is here attracting a honey bee and makes a delicate inset for this rosewood trinket box.

FLORAL TRINKET BOX

YOU WILL NEED

For the Trinket Box, with a lid measuring 10cm (4in) in diameter:

15cm (6in) square of cream, 18-count Aida fabric
15cm (6in) square of iron-on interfacing
Stranded embroidery cotton in the colours
given in the panel
No26 tapestry needle
A trinket box; these are available in wood, hand-cut lead or crystal, silver-plate and porcelain, in a variety of colours (for suppliers, see page 256) — you may wish to choose a bowl in a colour to match one of the colours in the embroidery

●

THE EMBROIDERY

Find the centre point on your square of Aida and, beginning from the centre of the pattern, embroider the flower motif, using two strands of cotton in the needle for the cross stitch and for all the backstitching in green. For the delicate backstitching on the bee's wings and body, use only one thread.

When working the cross stitch on the bee's wings, a thread of stranded cotton together with a strand of Kreinik Blending Filament was used. This gives the wings a translucent appearance.

Gently steam press the completed embroidery on the reverse side, but make sure that the iron does not come into direct contact with the blending filament.

ASSEMBLING THE TRINKET BOX

Iron the interfacing to the back of the embroidery. Take the acetate inset from the lid of your bowl and place it over the embroidery. This will enable you to place the motif centally within the circular space available. Using the acetate as a template, draw around it with a soft pencil. Cut carefully around the circle with a sharp pair of scissors, and complete the assembly, following the manufacturer's instructions.

▶ NIGELLA	DMC	ANCHOR	MADEIRA
⊥ Grey	413	401	1713
∷ Pale grey	762	234	1804
+BF100 (Kreinik Blending Filament 100)			
Z Yellow brown	783	307	2211
◥ Yellow	726	295	0109
‖ Light yellow brown	676	891	2208
◣ Navy	823	150	1008
□ Light navy	791	941	0904
⊠ Pale blue	794	175	0907
⚌ Very pale blue	800	129	0908
↓ Dark blue	792	940	0905
∧ Blue	793	121	0906
⊏ Dark green	580	267	1608
⎍ Green	581	266	1609
⍺ Pale green	472	264	1414

Note: Backstitch bee's body in yellow brown, stamens in green, bee's wings, legs and antennae in grey, the centre of the flower in navy, and the leaves in dark green.

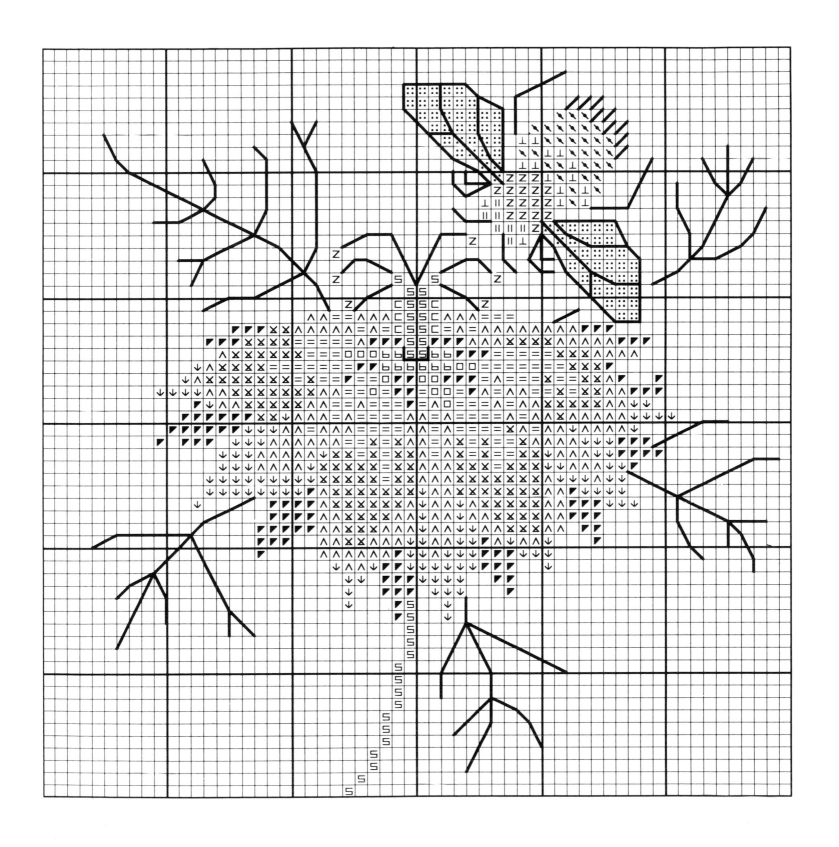

Lavender Gifts

The scent of lavender will permeate cupboards and drawers while its beauty can decorate your room all year round. These simple designs can be adapted to almost any project.

LAVENDER GIFTS

YOU WILL NEED

For a Lavender Bag, measuring approximately
14cm x 7.5cm (5¼in x 3in):

*21cm x 19.5cm 8½in x 7½in of 28-count violet
evenweave fabric
Stranded cotton in the colours given in the panel
No24 tapestry needle
30cm (12in) of violet ribbon, 1cm (⅜in) wide
Sewing thread to match the fabric
Dried lavender or pot pourri, for filling*

For a Drawer Scenter measuring
10cm (4in) square:

*15cm (6in) square of evenweave fabric, plus needle,
threads, and filling, as above
12.5cm (5in) square of printed cotton, for the back
1 7.5cm (7in) of violet ribbon, 1cm (⅜in) wide
Matching sewing thread*

For the Make-up Bag, measuring 16cm x 12.5cm
(6¼in x 5in):

*Ready-made bag in 28-count evenweave (the colour used
is English Rose, for suppliers see page 256)
Needle and threads, as above*

For the Trinket Box, with a lid measuring 5.5cm
(2⅛in) in diameter:

*15cm (6in) square of 14-count, white Aida fabric
Needle and threads, (as above)
Trinket box, for suppliers see page 256*

Note: If you are only stitching the Lavender Row
design, you will not require dark pink embroidery
cotton; for Lavender Bunch, you will not require
silver green, and for Lavender Posy, you will not
require pale pink, dark green and dark pink.

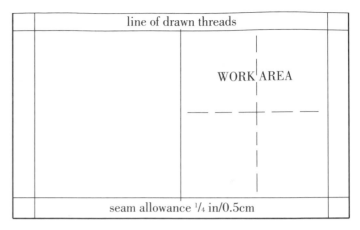

LAVENDER BAG

The diagram shows the trimmed fabric, but the
fabric quantity, gives an additional allowance of
2.5cm (1in) all around. Using basting stitches,
mark off the work area, 3cm (1¼in) up from the
lower edge of the fabric and the same in from each
side. Mark down the centre of the fabric – the
right-hand side is the work area. Mark a horizontal
line 7.5cm (3in) up from the. lower line of basting,
and a second line 1cm (⅜in) above it. Mark the centre of the enclosed work area with basting stitches
and set the fabric in a hoop.

Embroider the design, using two strands of
thread in the needle for the cross stitches and a single strand for the backstitch and taking each stitch
over two threads of the fabric.

When you have finished the embroidery, trim
the fabric to measure 16cm x 14.5cm (6½in x
5½in) and carefully remove all horizontal threads
from between the two upper horizontal lines of
basting stitches. Fold the fabric down the centre,
right sides together, and stitch the bottom and side
edges, taking a 6mm (½in) seam allowance. Turn
the bag right side out and remove horizontal
threads from the top 12mm (½in), to make a
fringe. Thread ribbon through the drawn-thread
area, over 10 and then under 5 threads, starting
and finishing at the seam. Fill the bag with lavender, then draw the ribbon and tie it in a bow.

DRAWER SCENTER

Mark the centre of the fabric with basting stitches
and embroider the design, using two strands of
thread in the needle for the cross stitches and a single
strand for the backstitch and taking each stitch over
two threads of the fabric. Trim the finished embroidery to measure 12.5cm (5in) square. Fold the ribbon
in half and pin it to lie over the front side, with the

fold to the centre and the ends at one corner. With right sides together, lay the printed cotton over the embroidery and loop and stitch around three sides, leaving a gap of 5cm (2in) in the remaining side and taking a 12mm (½in) seam allowance. Turn the fabric right side out; fill with lavender and then stitch the opening together neatly.

MAKE-UP BAG

Mark the centre of your work in the usual way. You cannot use a hoop, but this does not matter for a small piece of embroidery. Embroider the design, as for the lavender bag, repeating stems until you reach the required width (stop about 6mm/¼in short of the seams). When you have finished, stitch the lining together and push it back inside the pouch. As a finishing touch, you can tie a short length of ribbon through the tongue of the zip.

LAVENDER		DMC	ANCHOR	MADEIRA
◆	Silver grey	452	232	1807
■	Violet	792	177	0903
▼	Lavender	793	176	0902
✕	Lilac	341	117	0901
◇	Pale pink	224	894	0813
●	Dark green	924	879	1205
⊘	Silver green	926	838	1310
▢	Dark pink	3733	75	0605

TRINKET BOX

Mark the centre of the fabric with basting stitches and set in a small hoop or hold it in the hand. Embroider the design, using two strands of thread in the needle throughout. Using the template provided and with the basting stitches as guidelines, mark the shape of the lid on the fabric and cut it out. Remove the basting stitches and mount the fabric in the lid, following the manufacturer's instructions.

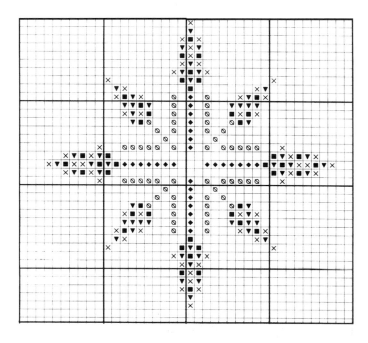

LAVENDER POSY

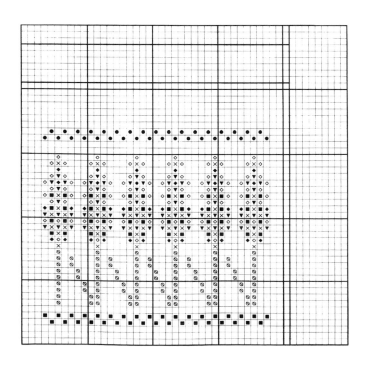

LAVENDER ROW

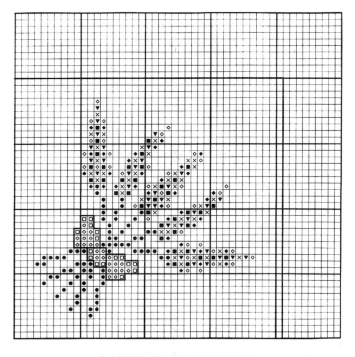

LAVENDER BUNCH

Peacock Needlework Box

Their magnificent tail feathers and iridescent colours made peacocks a natural subject for Art Nouveau. Shiny threads and beads combine to recreate this elegant design.

PEACOCK NEEDLEWORK BOX

YOU WILL NEED

For the Needlework Box, with a design area measuring 21cm x 17.5cm (8⅜in x 7in):

38cm x 33cm (15in x 13in) of apricot, 28-count eavenweave fabric
Stranded embroidery cotton and specialist thread in the colours listed in the panel
No26 tapestry needle
Seed beads in the colour listed in the panel

•

THE EMBROIDERY

Prepare the fabric and find the centre point (see *Basic Skills* pages 8–11). Some areas of the design require stranded cotton and rayon blending filament to be blended. Using two strands of cotton and one of blending filament, follow the instructions in *Basic Skills* (pages 8–11) for working with specialist threads. Work over two threads of the fabric and complete all the cross stitching following the chart. Backstitch the outlines as stated on the thread key. Finally, attach beads where shown by the symbols, (see *Basic Skills* pages 8–11).

FINISHING

Remove the embroidery from the frame and wash, if necessary, taking care with the beads. Lightly press the embroidery on the reverse side (avoid using steam as this can affect metallic threads). Assemble the box lid according to the manufacturer's instructions. Alternatively, this piece would be equally suitable framed as a picture.

► PEACOCK	DMC	ANCHOR	MADEIRA	MARLITT/ KREINIK
▼ Dark purple x 1 plus purple rayon x 1	550	101	0714	819
◇ Medium purple x 1 plus light purple rayon x 1	552	99	0715	858
▢ Turquoise	597	168	1110	–
⣈ Gold	783	307	2211	–
● Dark brown	838	380	2005	–
▯ Dark orange	918	341	0314	–
▼ Orange	922	1003	0310	–
⊠ Terracotta	975	355	2303	–
⊟ Dark green x 1 plus turquoise rayon x 1	991	189	1204	1053
⠇⠇ Olive	3011	845	1607	–
♡ Light olive	3013	842	1605	–
S Dark turquoise x 1 plus purple rayon x 1	3808	170	2508	819
■ Dark turquoise	3808	170	2508	–
X Medium turquoise	3809	169	2507	–
— Aqua x 1 plus dark turquoise rayon x 1	3814	187	1203	1056
Aquamarine (Kreinik)*	–	–	–	Kreinik No.8 Braid 242 HL
Magenta (Kreinik)*	–	–	–	Kreinik No.8 Braid 242 HL
▣ Deep blue beads	V3.04.930	–	–	–

Note: Backstitch outer edges of large 'eyes' in tail feathers, feather quills on head, and those attaching large 'eye' feathers to tail with Kreinik Aquamarine. Backstitch purple and turquoise centres of large 'eyes' (referring to photograph if necessary) with Kreinik Magenta* (*used for backstitch only).*

151

Pot Pourri Delights

Enhance your bedroom with these rose fan designs for insertion into a crystal glass bowl, and the floral pot pourri sachets with their transparent inserts. Both designs are worked in a choice of two colourways to match your decor.

POT POURRI DELIGHTS

YOU WILL NEED

For the Bowl Lid, with an insert measuring 9cm (3½in) in diameter:

14cm (5½in) square of white, 26-count evenweave linen
Stranded embroidery cotton in the colours given in the appropriate panel
No24 tapestry needle
Crystal bowl with prepared lid
(for suppliers, see page 256)

For the Pot Pourri Sachet, with a design size measuring 15cm (6in) square:

20cm (8in) square of white, 26-count evenweave linen
Stranded embroidery cotton in the colours given in the appropriate panel
No24 tapestry needle
20cm (8in) square of fusible web
Fabric adhesive
10cm (4in) square of white muslin
20cm (8in) square of white cotton fabric
Matching sewing thread
Pot pourri of your choice
4 ribbon roses in a matching colour

●

THE BOWL

Prepare the fabric and stretch it in a hoop (see *Basic Skills* pages 8–11). Mark the central horizontal and vertical lines on the fabric with basting stitches. Following the correct chart, start stitching at the centre of the design using two strands of embroidery thread in the needle, except for the background of the fan which is worked in one strand. Work the cross stitch over two threads of fabric in each direction. Make sure that all the top crosses run in the same direction and that each row is worked into the top or bottom of the row before. Backstitch the base of the fan using one strand of thread, and backstitch the tassel using two strands.

Remove from the hoop and steam press. Assemble the lid following the manufacturer's instructions.

THE POT POURRI SACHET

Prepare the fabric and stretch it in a hoop (see *Basic Skills* pages 8–11). Mark the central horizontal and vertical lines of the fabric with basting stitches. Start at the centre of the design, using two strands of embroidery thread in the needle. Work the cross stitch over two threads of fabric in each direction. Work the backstitch with one strand of thread in the needle.

Remove the finished embroidery from the hoop and steam press it on the reverse side. Iron the square of fusible web on to the reverse side of the embroidery. Remove the backing paper and carefully cut a square of fabric from the centre of the embroidery, 12mm (½in) from the inside line of cross stitching. Apply fabric adhesive around the edges of the opening on the wrong side and stick the square of muslin firmly in place. Allow to dry.

Place the embroidery and white cotton fabric together, right sides facing, and baste and machine stitch together, 12mm (½in) from the edge. Leave an opening of 5cm (2in) for turning. Trim the corners and turn the sachet to the right side. Fill with pot pourri and sew up. Stitch a ribbon rose to each corner.

► PINK ROSE FAN		DMC	ANCHOR	MADEIRA
+	Light gold	745	386	0111
−	Light gold (1 strand only)	745	386	0111
⊡	Dark pink	962	52	0505
⊙	Light pink	963	24	0607
T	Dark green	3051	845	1508
Ǝ	Green	3052	844	1509
⊿	Light green	3348	264	1409
∧	Pink	3716	25	0606
■	Dark gold	3822	305	0110

Note: Backstitch base of fan in dark green; backstitch tassel thread in dark gold (2 strands).

► YELLOW ROSE FAN		DMC	ANCHOR	MADEIRA
⊙	Light yellow	727	293	0103
⊡	Dark yellow	742	302	0107
V	Yellow	744	300	0110
+	Light gold	745	386	0111
−	Light gold (1 strand only)	745	386	0111
T	Dark green	3051	845	1508
Ǝ	Green	3052	844	1509
⊿	Light green	3348	264	1409
■	Dark gold	3822	305	0110

Note: Backstitch base of fan in dark green; backstitch tassel thread in dark gold (2 strands).

154

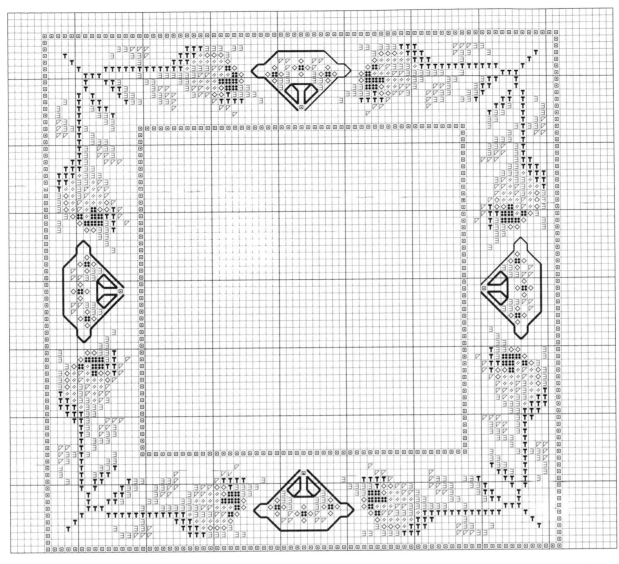

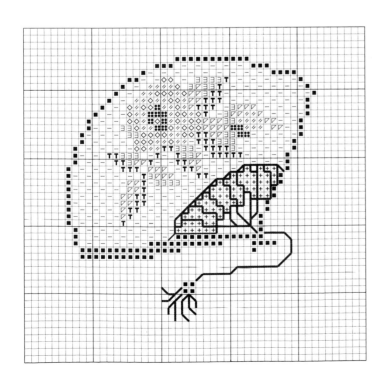

▲ PINK ROSE SACHET		DMC	ANCHOR	MADEIRA
⣏	Dark pink	962	52	0505
◇	Light pink	963	24	0607
⧄	Pink	3716	25	0606
T	Dark green	3051	845	1508
Ⴈ	Green	3052	844	1509
◺	Light green	3348	264	1409
⊡	Dark gold	3822	305	0110

Note: Backstitch outlines in dark green.

▲ YELLOW ROSE SACHET		DMC	ANCHOR	MADEIRA
◇	Light yellow	727	293	0103
⧄	Yellow	744	300	0110
⣏	Dark yellow	742	302	0107
T	Dark green	3051	845	1508
Ⴈ	Green	3052	844	1509
◺	Light green	3348	264	1409
⊡	Dark gold	3822	305	0110

Note: Backstitch outlines in dark green.

Luxury Linens

Tablecloths, place mats and towels provide a blank canvas that just cries out to be decorated with designs such as the nasturtium borders, butterfly garlands and cheery lazy daisy featured here.

NASTURTIUM TABLE LINEN

YOU WILL NEED

For each Table Mat, measuring
30cm (12in) square:

*33cm (13in) square of antique cream, 28-count
evenweave fabric
Stranded embroidery cotton in the colours listed in the
appropriate panel
No26 tapestry needle
30cm (12in) square of white or cream cotton for
backing
Matching sewing thread*

●

THE EMBROIDERY

Prepare the fabric and find the centre (see *Basic Skills* pages 8–11); this will help with the placement of the borders. Decide how far from the edge of the fabric you wish to start your border, allowing for a hem of approximately 12mm (½in). You may wish to run a line of light basting stitches to indicate the start and finish of your border.

Use the pattern repeat to decide how many repeats will comfortably fit on your fabric. When ready to stitch, start from the centre of the pattern repeat. Using two strands of thread in the needle and stitching over two threads of the fabric, complete all the cross stitching following the chart. Work the backstitching using one strand of thread in the needle.

In order to stitch the horizontal border in the toning colourway, replace the dark and medium green in the leaves with brown; medium green in the stems and buds with dark brown; the dark orange with medium brown; and the light orange with light brown.

To stitch the vertical border in the bright colourway, replace light brown with light orange; dark brown with dark green; brown with medium green; and medium brown with dark orange.

Note that the bright colourway has five shades and the toning colourway only four. The centre of the flowers are stitched in dark brown in both colour options.

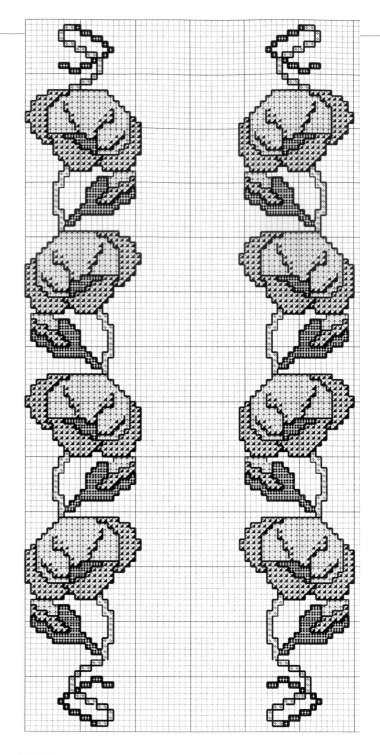

▲ ▶ VERTICAL NASTURTIUMS	DMC	ANCHOR	MADEIRA
Toning colourway			
◢ Brown	400	351	2305
↑ Light brown	402	1047	2307
⠿ Dark brown	938	381	2005
◥ Medium brown	3776	1048	1105
Bright colourway			
◢ Medium green	471	266	1501
↑ Light orange	741	304	0201
⠿ Dark green	469	267	1503
◥ Dark orange	608	332	0205
▼ Dark brown	938	381	2005

Note: Backstitch outlines in dark brown.

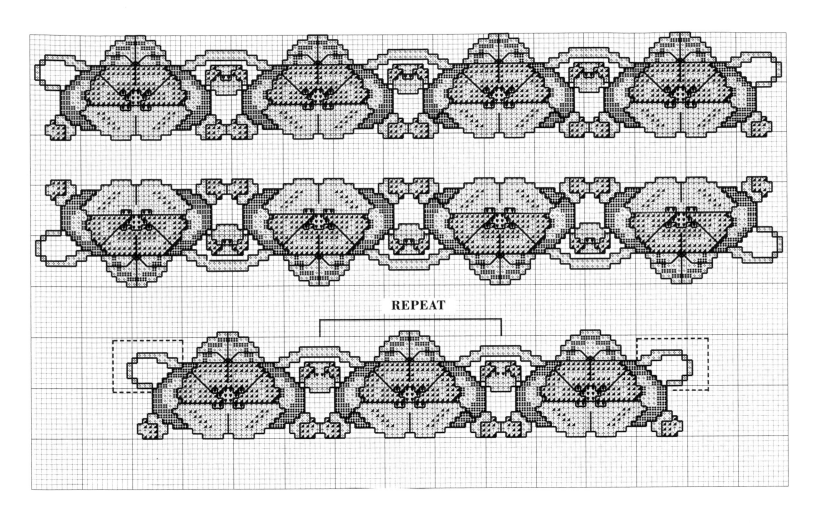

REPEAT

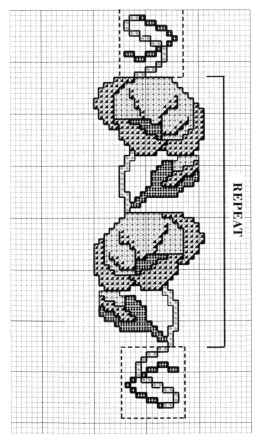

REPEAT

▲ HORIZONTAL NASTURTIUMS		DMC	ANCHOR	MADEIRA
Bright colourway				
⊞	Dark green	469	267	1503
◹	Medium green	471	266	1501
◿	Dark orange	608	332	0205
↑	Light orange	741	304	0201
▼	Dark brown	938	381	2005
Toning colourway				
◹	Brown	400	351	2305
⊞	Dark brown	938	381	2005
◿	Medium brown	3776	1048	1105
↑	Light brown	402	1047	2307

Note: Backstitch outlines in dark brown.

FINISHING

Remove the embroidery from the frame. Turn and press a 12mm (½in) hem all around the stitched piece. With the reverse sides together, place the stitched piece on to the backing fabric. Turn the hem edges on to the backing, slipstitch into place, and press gently.

Butterflies and Bows

Brighten your towels with these attractive swags and decorate the bathroom door by stitching a useful fingerplate to match. The spiral garland can be lengthened or shortened and worked vertically or horizontally to fit your linen.

BUTTERFLIES AND BOWS

YOU WILL NEED

For the Finger Plate, measuring 25.5cm x 6.5cm (1in x 2½in) :

30cm x 11cm (12in x 4½in) of 14-count Aida Plus fabric, in white (ordinary Aida fabric could be used, but the stiffness of Aida Plus makes assembly of the finger plate easier)
Stranded embroidery cotton in the colours given in the appropriate panel
No26 tapestry needle
Finger plate, as specified above
(for stockists, see page 256)

For either of the Towel Bands, each of which measures approximately 51cm x 86cm (20in x 34in), with repeats as used here:

55cm (21½in) of 15-count Aida band, 5cm (2in) wide, white with white edging
Stranded embroidery cotton in the colours given in the appropriate panel
No26 tapestry needle
Hand towel in the colour of your choice for the spiral design and white for the pansy swag design

●

FINGER PLATE

For the finger plate, mark the centre lines on the Aida Plus fabric with basting stitches. Work the cross stitch with two strands of thread and the back stitch and French knots with one strand. Steam press the completed embroidery on the reverse side.

If using Aida Plus, cover the reverse side with a cloth to prevent the backing from sticking to the iron. Assemble the finger plate according to the manufacturer's instructions.

TOWEL BANDS

Towels vary in width, but both designs can easily be adjusted to fit most hand towel sizes. Make sure that your Aida band is sufficiently long to run across the width of the towel and leave a 12mm (½in) allowance, for turning, at each end.

For each towel band, mark the centre with basting stitches. It is important to begin stitching at the centre of the Aida band. For the pansy swag border, stitch the central swag first and then repeat the swag design on each side, counting 14 blocks between each swag. Embroider the cross stitches first, using two strands of thread in the needle, and then work the backstitches and French knots, this time using one strand in the needle.

FLOWER AND RIBBON SPIRALS		DMC	ANCHOR	MADEIRA
◇	Yellow	444	291	0106
▽	Blue	518	1039	1106
↑	Pale blue	519	1038	1105
K	Purple	552	100	0805
X	Dark pink	601	63	0703
+	Pink	604	55	0614
Y	Orange	740	316	0202
＼	Very pale blue	747	158	1104
S	Gold	783	307	2211
▼	Dark green	909	923	1303
∃	Medium green	911	205	1214
⊐	Light green	913	204	1212
H	Brown	3790	393	1905
∧	Light gold	3820	305	0108

Note: Backstitch butterfly legs and antennae with brown, adding a brown French knot to the end of each antenna.

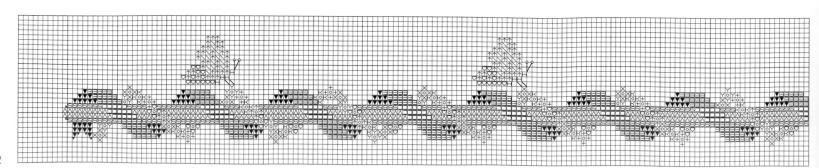

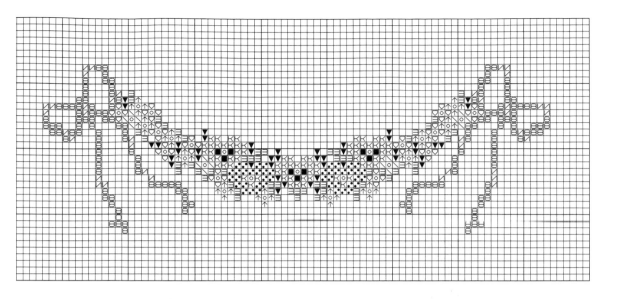

▲ PANSY SWAG		DMC	ANCHOR	MADEIRA
■	Black	310	403	Black
O	Yellow	444	291	0106
♡	Blue	518	1039	1106
↑	Pale blue	519	1038	1105
K	Purple	552	100	0805
⋰	Lilac	554	96	0711
8	Red	666	46	0210
＼	Very pale blue	747	158	1104
▼	Dark green	909	923	1303
Ε	Medium green	911	205	1214
И	Light red	3705	35	0411

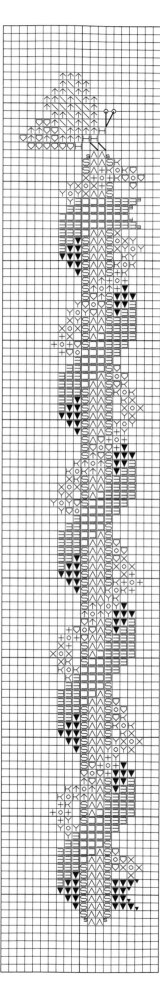

Steam press the completed embroidery on the reverse side. At each short end of the band, form and press a turning (checking that the finished length fits your towel neatly). Most towels have a strip of flatly woven fabric a few centimetres from each end, and the Aida band can be pinned and basted to one of these strips. Using matching thread and, stitching close to all edges of the Aida band, stitch it in place.

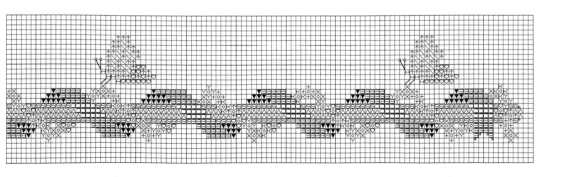

Cottage Garden Table Set

This colourful project will bring summer flowers to your table all the year around. Both the place mat and the pair of coasters are quick to make and suitable for beginners.

COTTAGE GARDEN TABLE SET

YOU WILL NEED

For the Place Mat, with a finished size of 35cm x 29cm (14in x 11½in):

41cm x 33cm (16in x 13in) of ivory 28-count evenweave fabric
Stranded embroidery cotton in the colours given in the panel
No24 and No26 tapestry needles

For the Coasters, with a design area measuring 6.5cm (2½in) square:

35cm x 18cm (14in x 7¼in) of white 18-count Aida fabric
Stranded embroidery cotton in the colours given in the panel
No26 tapestry needle
Cream embroidery thread
Acrylic coaster, 8cm (3¼in) round
Acrylic coaster, 8cm (3¼in) square

●

THE PLACE MAT

First, prepare the fabric, basting the horizontal and vertical centre lines, (see *Basic Skills* pages 8–11). Set the fabric in a hoop or frame (see *Basic Skills* pages 8–11), and begin stitching from the centre, following the chart. Ensure that the long axis of the fabric is running horizontally.

Work the cross stitch using two strands of thread in the No24 tapestry needle, and working over two threads of the fabric in each direction to form a cross stitch. Make sure that all the top stitches run in the same direction. Work the backstitch using one strand of thread and the No26 needle.

HEMSTITCHING

To finish the place mat, remove the embroidery from the frame. Trim the fabric to the finished size, being careful to remove an equal amount of fabric from each of the four sides. Count twelve threads in from the raw edges, and remove one thread on each

▶ PLACE MAT		ANCHOR	DMC	MADEIRA
2	Light salmon pink	1022	760	0405
3	Dark salmon pink	1023	3712	0406
↑	Pale yellow	293	727	0110
⌐	Sand	373	3828	2102
E	Dark sand	374	420	2103
H	Maroon	43	815	0513
L	Medium green	266	3347	1408
O	Bright yellow	295	726	0100
/	Light grey green	875	503	1702
S	Dark grey green	876	502	1703
T	Bright green	241	954	1211
V	Brick	883	3064	2312
N	Grey blue	849	927	1708
Z	Dark blue	851	924	1706
+	Purple	98	553	0712
	Dark brown*	381	838	1914

Note: Backstitch flower detail with maroon, and cottage detail, including windows, with dark brown* (*used for backstitch only); follow the small chart showing large cross stitches.

▶ COASTERS		ANCHOR	DMC	MADEIRA
•	Light stone	391	3024	1901
2	Dark brick	883	3064	2312
3	Light brick	882	3773	2313
S	Grey blue	850	926	1707
E	Grey brown	903	3032	2002
=	Dark grey	8581	646	1812
↑	Light grey	900	648	1814
⌐	Light grey*	900	648	1814
H	Dark green	217	319	1313
L	Medium green	215	320	1311
N	Pink	50	3716	0612
T	Light yellow	293	727	0110
V	Light sage green	262	3051	1508
Z	Dark pink	42	961	0610
Y	Dark blue	851	924	1706

Note: Backstitch details with one strand of dark grey. Work smoke in light grey* using tent stitch (*tent stitch only).

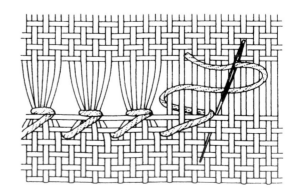

▲ PLACE MAT

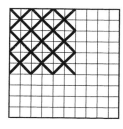

▲ BACKSTITCH
WINDOW DESIGN

COASTERS ►

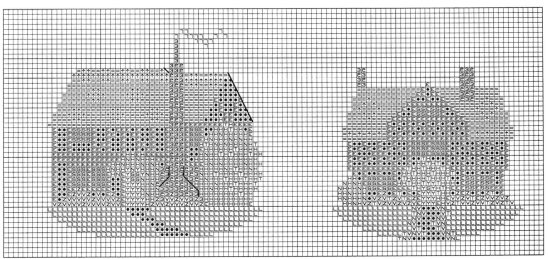

of the four sides. This forms the hem line. Take two strands of cream embroidery thread in the No24 needle and begin to hem as follows.

Starting from the bottom left-hand corner, bring the needle out on the right side of the work, four threads inside the drawn thread line. Working from left to right, pick up four threads. Bring the needle out again and insert it behind the fabric to emerge four threads along ready to make the next stitch. Before inserting the needle, pull the thread tight, so that the bound threads form a neat group.

When you have finished hemstitching, pull away the threads outside the hem to produce a frayed edge.

THE COASTERS

Prepare the fabric by dividing it into two squares measuring 18cm (7¼in) each, and centring them as before. Set in a hoop or frame and stitch from the centre. Work all stitches with one strand of thread in the No26 needle. Trim the fabric to fit the coaster, and assemble as shown in the instructions.

Rose Corner

Romance could certainly be in the air with this beautiful tablecloth, embroidered with a ring of red roses and accompanied by a matching crystal bowl and silver-framed picture. This set will brighten up a corner of the darkest room, and if the bowl is filled with pot pourri, it will provide a lingering fragrance of summer to complete the effect.

ROSE CORNER

YOU WILL NEED

For the Tablecloth, measuring approximately
1m (39in) square:

*90cm (36in) square of white Lugana fabric, with
25 threads to 2.5cm (1in)
Stranded embroidery cotton in the colours in the panel
3m (3½yds) of gathered lace, 9cm (3½in) wide
No24 tapestry needle*

For the Bowl Lid, with an inset measuring 9cm
(3½in) in diameter:

*14cm (5½in) square of Zweigart's white 14-count
Aida fabric
Stranded embroidery cotton in the colours in the panel
No24 tapestry needle
Crystal bowl with prepared lid
(for suppliers, see page 256)*

For the Picture, in an oval frame measuring
8cm x 10cm (3in x 4in):

*13cm x 15cm (5in x 6in) of Zweigart's white
14-count Aida fabric
Stranded embroidery cotton in the colours in the panel
No24 tapestry needle
Oval frame (for suppliers, see page 256)*

●

THE TABLECLOTH

Prepare the linen and stretch it in a hoop (see *Basic Skills* pages 8–11). Alternatively, as the evenweave linen is a firmly-woven fabric, it is possible to embroider without a hoop. Following the chart, begin with the central circle, then work outward. Use two strands of embroidery cotton in the needle throughout, and work each stitch over two threads of fabric in each direction.

MAKING UP

Stain press on the wrong side. Make a hem 12mm (½in) deep around the outside of the cloth, mitring the corners (see *Basic Skills* pages 8–11). Next,

measure 24cm (9½in) in each side from each corner and lightly mark the right side of the cloth with a soft pencil, 12mm (½in) in from the edge.

Pin and baste the gathered lace to the tablecloth, positioning the straight edge of the lace 12mm (½in) in from the edge. When you reach the pencil marks, baste the lace across the corner of the cloth, between the two marks. Slipstitch the lace in place.

BOWL LID AND PICTURE

For each, prepare the fabric, basting the central vertical and horizontal lines, and set it in a hoop (see *Basic Skills* pages 8–11). Use two strands of embroidery cotton in the needle and work over one block of fabric in each direction. Start at the centre of the work and work outward. Steam press the finished work and mount it as explained in the manufacturer's instructions.

PICTURE ▶

BOWL LID ▼

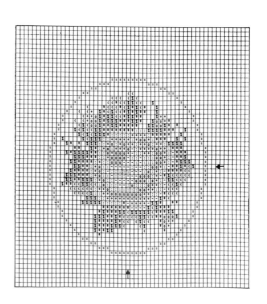

TABLECLOTH ▲

▲ RED ROSE TABLECLOTH BOWL AND PICTURE	DMC	ANCHOR	MADEIRA			DMC	ANCHOR	MADEIRA
─ Pink	892	28	0413		< Light green	369	213	1309
: Light red	666	46	0210		% Medium green	368	214	1310
+ Medium red	304	42	0511		‡ Dark green	367	216	1312
O Dark red	814	44	0514		= Grey	415	398	1803

Note: One skein of each colour is sufficient for all three designs.

Lazy Daisy Bathroom Set

Brighten up your bathroom with ever-popular daisies. These quick, versatile designs would look equally good as a colourful trim for bed linen and curtains.

LAZY DAISY
BATHROOM SET

YOU WILL NEED

14-count canvas (for suppliers see page 256) – the
canvas should always be at least 2.5cm (1in) larger
each way than the finished motif(s)
Stranded embroidery cotton in the colours
given in the panel
Sharp needle
Items of your choice

Note: for best results, use items made from non-stretch fabrics; you can, if preferred, decorate the towels with strips of Aida band, embroidered with the repeat motifs, instead of using the waste canvas technique to embroider directly on the towels.

•

WASH BAG AND SLIPPERS

For the wash bag, cut a 10cm (4in) square of waste canvas. Centre the canvas over the area where the motif is to be stitched and pin it in position; use the blue threads in the canvas to ensure that the finished embroidery lies straight on the bag, aligning it either with the weave of the fabric or with the pattern (if any). Start the design from the centre, treating each pair of canvas threads as one. The pins may be removed after a few stitches have secured the canvas to the bag.

Following the chart, cross stitch in the usual manner, using three strands of thread in a sharp-pointed needle. Take care to stitch through the holes and not the canvas, as the latter would make it difficult to withdraw the threads.

Finally, stitch the petals of the daisies, this time using six strands of thread in the needle. The daisy petals are indicated on the chart by a straight line and are made by a single chain stitch (lazy daisy stitch). If you find this stitch difficult to work on the canvas, you may prefer to stitch it after the waste canvas has been removed. However, although it will be easier after removing the canvas, you will need to estimate the length of the stitches and make sure they are equal.

Exactly the same method is used to stitch the slippers. For these you will need two pieces of canvas, each 5cm (2in) square (one piece for each slipper). Please note that there are two separate designs, one for the left and the other for the right slipper. After pinning the waste canvas in position, follow the above instructions.

For the bath towels, you will need 3.5cm x 5cm (½in x 2in) and for the hand towels, a 3cm (1¼in) square of waste canvas for each motif. The design is repeated every 2.5cm (1in) on the hand towels and worked in groups of three (one set of three at each end and one in the centre) on the bath towel.

FINISHING

When you have finished the embroidery, cut away surplus canvas around the design. Dampen the right side with slightly warm water and leave it for a few minutes until the sizing in the canvas softens. Gently remove the canvas threads, one at a time, with tweezers. The threads should come out easily, but the operation requires patience; if you try to remove several threads at once, this could spoil your embroidery.

LAZY DAISY

Bring your needle out at the base of the petal shape; hold the thread down with your thumb as you reinsert the needle slightly to the right of the starting point. Bring the point of the needle out, inside the loop, at the required length of the stitch (petal); pull the thread through, and make a small stitch over the end of the loop, to hold it in place. Bring the needle out again at the base of the next stitch (petal).

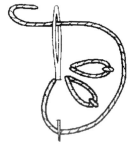 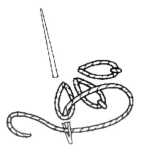

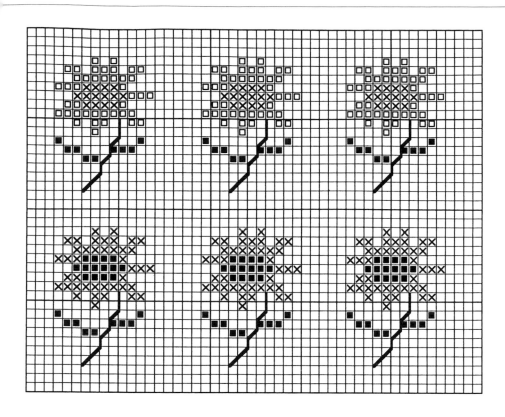

BATHTOWEL

SLIPPERS

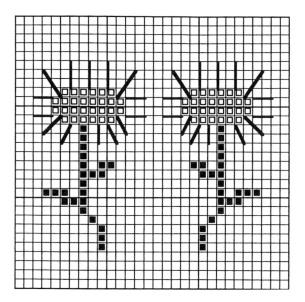

RIGHT   **LEFT**

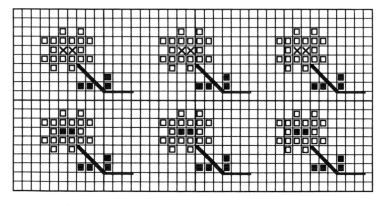

HAND TOWEL

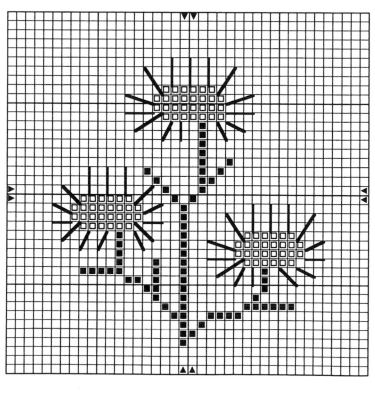

LAZY DAISIES	ANCHOR	DMC	MADEIRA
White	1	White	White
☐ Yellow	298	972	0107
☒ Red	46	666	0210
■ Green	238	703	1307

Note: Use all six strands of white thread for lazy daisy stitches; backstitch stem outlines using three strands of green thread.

WASH BAG

For a Golden Table

Add a golden sparkle to your table on special occasions, such as wedding anniversaries, with a set of either basil or nasturtium napkins, or a mixture of both, and nasturtium place cards, all stitched in gold thread.

FOR A GOLDEN TABLE

YOU WILL NEED

For each Napkin, of either the basil or nasturtium design, measuring 37.5cm (15in) square:

Either a ready-made napkin in a plain colour of your choice or a 40cm (16in) square of cotton, cotton/polyester or linen fabric
DMC Fil d'or or a similar gold embroidery thread
14-count waste canvas – 8cm x 10cm for each basil napkin or a 10cm (4in) square cut diagonally in half for two nasturtium napkins
No 6 crewel needle
Sewing thread
Laundry spray
Tweezers or fine Jeweller's pliers
Gold tassel (optional)

For each Place Card, measuring 10cm (4in) each way (maximum height):

10cm x 14cm (4in x 5½in) of Aida plus (or 14-count Aida and iron-on fabric stiffener cut to measure)
DMC Fil d'or or a similar gold embroidery thread
No24 tapestry needle

●

THE NAPKINS

If you are making your own napkins, first turn under and press a double 6mm (¼in) hem all around and machine stitch, close to the folded edge. If you are embroidering the basil napkin, baste the waste canvas at a 45 degree angle to one corner, and mark the centre of the canvas as you would if you were embroidering a piece of Aida fabric.

For a nasturtium napkin, baste the right angle of the canvas to the right angle of machine stitching at one corner; count up from the corner to start stitching the centre of the nasturtium flower 4.5cm (1½in) in from the corner. Embroider the design through both the canvas and the napkin fabric, using two strands of gold thread. Use very short lengths of this special thread to prevent it wearing out or becoming tarnished.

FINISHING THE NAPKIN

When the embroidery is complete, trim the excess canvas to about 12mm (½in) around the edges of your stitching. Now dampen the remainder with a laundry spray. The canvas will become damp and sticky. While it is in this state, gently but firmly pull the canvas threads from underneath the gold thread. It is a good idea to practise on those threads around the edge that have no embroidered stitches over them; in this way you will familiarize yourself with the feel of the damp canvas before tackling your precious stitches

Once all the canvas has been removed, your gold work will gleam on the fabric! Leave the napkins to dry naturally, or press on the reverse side with a clean cloth, over a soft towel to protect the stitching. These napkins can be hand washed, or machine washed on a gentle cycle. If you use starch, spray onto the reverse side only.

For the basil napkin, hand sew a running stitch along all four edges, using the gold thread and following the machine-stitched hem as a guide. Again using the gold thread, weave a second line under these stitches, producing a wavy line around the edge.

If you choose to finish each napkin with a tassel, use only a few stitches and make sure that it can easily be removed for laundering, when necessary.

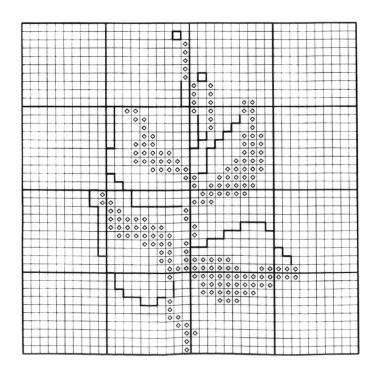

BASIL NAPKIN

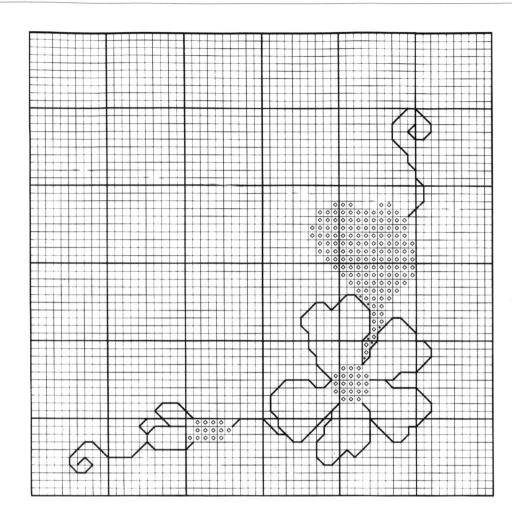

NASTURTIUM NAPKIN

PLACE CARDS

Stitch the design, following the chart in the usual way. If you are using Aida plus, it is not necessary to mount this in a hoop. When the stitching is finished, fold along the line marked on the chart.

Carefully cut from this fold around the leaves, stopping when you reach the fold on the other side of them. Now cut the slot as illustrated. Re-fold the card along the crease, leaving the cut-out part standing free. Iron on the reverse side.

Write the name of your guest on a piece of card and slip it into the slot. In this way you will be able to use your place cards over and over again.

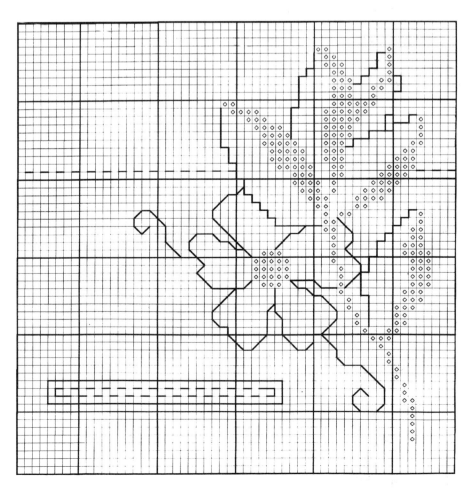

NASTURTIUM PLACE CARD

Crewel-style Place Setting

Worked in only six shades of blue, this garland combines the flowing curves and stylized leaves of 17th-century crewel work with the cool blues of traditional pottery designs, to create a look which is perfect for modern table linen.

CREWEL-STYLE PLACE SETTING

YOU WILL NEED

For the Table Napkin, measuring
28cm (15in) square:

*39cm square of 28-count Brittney evenweave fabric,
in white*
Stranded cotton in the colours given in the panel
No26 tapestry needle
Madeira rayon machine embroidery thread,
Art No 9840, shade 2016, blue mix
(for the satin-stitched hem)

Note: Madeira rayon machine embroidery thread
has been used for the edging. There is no exact
equivalent in the other brands listed, but you can
substitute other machine threads, provided you
obtain an attractive effect.

For the Placemat, measuring 28cm (11in) in
diameter:

*37.5cm (13in) square of 28-count Brittney evenweave
fabric, in white*
*Stranded embroidery cotton in the colours given in the
panel*
No26 tapestry needle
*37.5cm (13in) square of heat-proof felt wadding,
available from good needlework stockists*
37.5cm (13in) square of white backing fabric

●

THE TABLE NAPKIN

It is advisable to hem the napkin before beginning
to embroider the design. Fold, gently steam press
and baste in place a 12mm (½in) hem around all
the edges.

Mitre each corner by trimming about 6mm (¼in)
from the point, then folding in the remaining fabric diagonally, so that the foldline crosses the hem-
line at the corner; and then turning in the hem,
butting the folded edges together. Stitch the hem
in place by enclosing the raw edges with a narrow
machined satin stitch, using rayon machine
embroidery thread.

The napkin could be hemmed in other ways, but
for some methods such as fringing or traditional
drawn-thread edgings you would need to add an
extra hem allowance.

Work the embroidery in a corner of the napkin,
starting with the bottom right corner of the
design. Use two strands of thread over two threads
of the fabric for the cross stitches and then embroider the backstitches, this time using one strand of
thread over two threads of the fabric.

THE PLACEMAT

For each mat, prepare the fabric (see *Basic Skills*
pages 8–11), marking the centre lines with basting
stitches, and set it in a hoop or frame. Begin by
counting from the centre to the nearest convenient
point: the large central flower at the base of the
design is a good starting point. Use two strands of
thread over two threads of the fabric for the cross
stitches and then embroider the backstitches, now
using one strand of thread over two threads of the
fabric. Remove the finished embroidery from the
hoop or frame and steam press the embroidery on
the wrong side.

Keeping the design centred, a circle 30cm (12in)
in diameter on the embroidered fabric, the
wadding and backing fabric. To do this, use the
inside line of a 30cm (12in) embroidery hoop as a
template, drawing the lines with a yellow quilter's
marking pencil. Cut out each circle; place the
embroidered fabric and backing fabric with right
sides together, and then put the wadding on top of
the reverse side of embroidery. Baste the pieces
together, then machine stitch, 12mm (½in) from
the edge, leaving an opening of 7.5cm (3in) for
turning through.

Trim the wadding close to the stitching and trim
the remaining seam allowances back to 6mm (¼in).
Gently, easing it into shape, turn the placemat
through to the right side. Close the opening with
slipstitching. Place the embroidered side of the
mat face down on a thick towel and press gently,
making sure the edges curve smoothly into a circle.

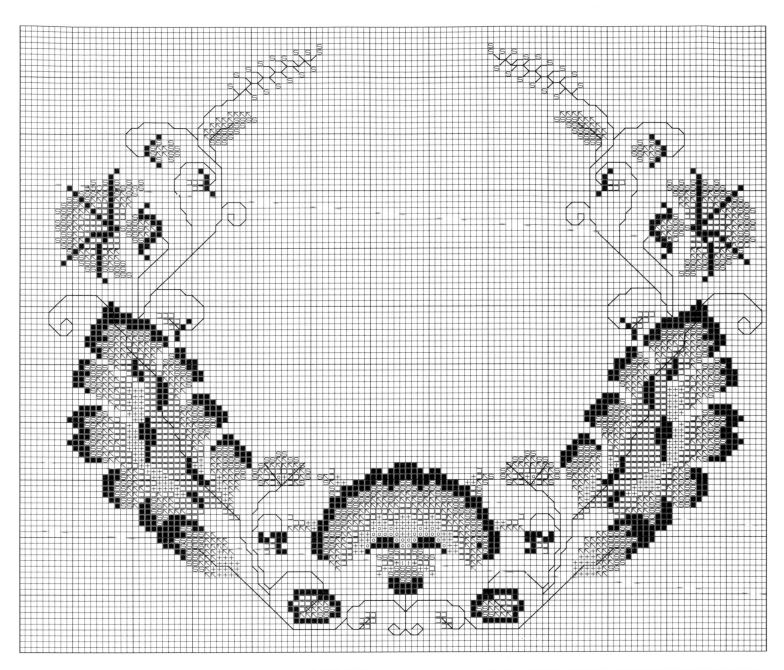

▲ ▶ BLUE GARLAND			
	DMC	**ANCHOR**	**MADEIRA**
■ Dark navy blue	336	150	1007
+ Powder blue	775	128	1001
S Royal blue	797	132	0912
⅃ Light blue	800	144	0908
↖ Medium blue	809	130	0909
O Ice blue	3756	1037	1104

Note: Embroider all backstitch details with one strand of dark navy blue.

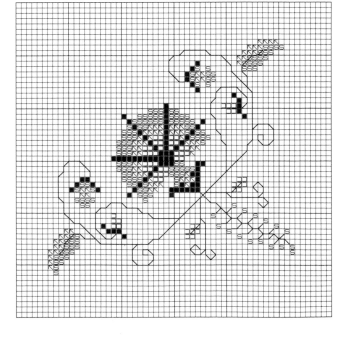

Hydrangea Tea Cosy

This elegant tea cosy embroidered with lace-cap hydrangeas in delicate pastel shades, will make teatime extra special. Alternatively, you might like to stitch this attractive design as a framed picture, perhaps using fabric with a higher count.

Pansies and Roses

This delightful placemat and napkin will certainly enhance any table setting, whether for a candlelit dinner or a summer party. You might vary the shades of the roses and pansies to match either your table setting, or perhaps the flowers from your own garden. If you want to change the design to make up an alternative set, you could quite easily adapt the motif to fit a corner instead of running down the side.

PANSIES AND ROSES

YOU WILL NEED

For one Placemat, measuring 33cm x 47cm
(13in x 19in), and one Napkin, measuring 40cm,
(16in) square:

Ready-prepared placemat and napkin
(for suppliers, see page 256), 26 threads to 2.5cm (1in)
Stranded embroidery cotton in the colours given
in the panel
No24 tapestry needle

Note: If you prefer not to use ready-prepared table
linen, buy fabric with the same thread count.
Work the embroidery first; trim to the correct
size (including fringe), and withdraw a thread
12mm (½in) in from each edge. Neatly overcast
every alternate thread, and then remove all
cross threads below the stitched line to complete
the fringe.

PREPARING THE FABRIC

First mark the centre (horizontal) line along the
length of the placemat with a line of basting stitches. Measure in 2.5cm (1in) from the start of the
fringe on the right-hand side and make a vertical
line of basting stitches. Position the centre of the
motif on the horizontal line of basting stitches and
the right-hand edge of the motif along the vertical
line of basting stitches. For the napkin, measure in
and baste lines 12mm (½in) in from the edge, at
one corner, as base lines for positioning.

Stretch the placemat or napkin in a frame (see
Basic Skills pages 8–11).

THE EMBROIDERY

Start at the centre of the appropriate motif and,
using two strands of embroidery cotton in the needle, work each stitch over two threads of fabric in
each direction. Make sure that all the top crosses
run in the same direction and that each row is
worked into the same holes as the top or bottom of
the preceding row, so that you do not leave a space
between rows.

Gently steam press the finished work on the
reverse side to remove all creases.

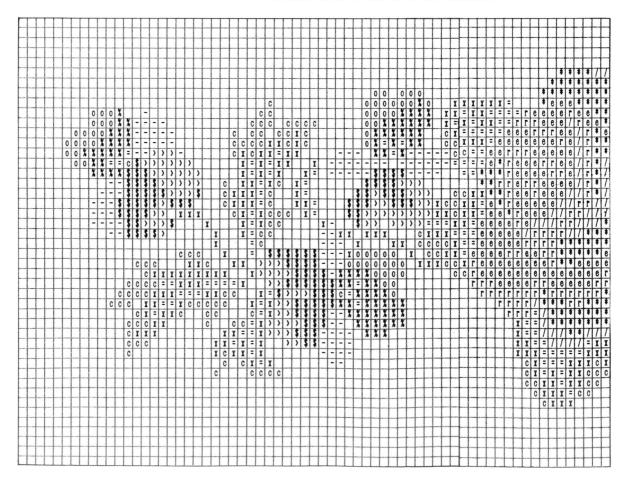

PANSIES AND ROSES

		DMC	ANCHOR	MADEIRA
‡	Light pink	3609	85	0710
/	Medium pink	3608	86	0709
r	Dark pink	718	88	0707
e	Darkest pink	915	89	0705
—	Light mauve	210	108	0803
>	Medium mauve	208	111	0804
S	Dark mauve	562	210	1202
%	Light yellow	3078	292	0102
O	Dark yellow	743	301	0113
C	Light green	3052	844	1509
X	Medium green	3347	266	1408
=	Dark green	3051	845	1508

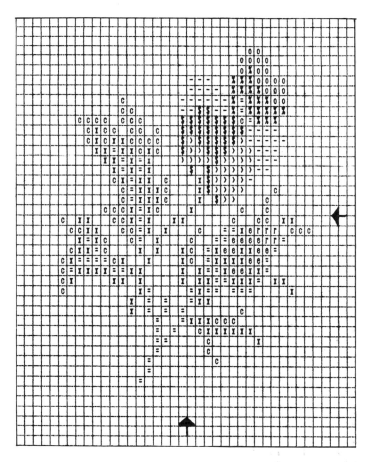

Periwinkle Table Set

This place setting and matching napkin are decorated with an attractive periwinkle design and will enhance any dining table.

PERIWINKLE TABLE SET

YOU WILL NEED

For one Placemat, measuring 46cm x 34cm (18½in x 13½in):

50cm x 39cm (20in x 15½in) of cream, 28-count evenweave fabric
Stranded embroidery cotton in the colours given in the panel
No26 tapestry needle

For one Napkin, measuring 37cm (14½in) square:

42cm (16½in) square of cream, 28-count evenweave fabric
Stranded embroidery cotton in the colours given in the panel
No26 tapestry needle

Note: alternatively, ready-made placemats and napkins can be obtained from specialist suppliers (see page 256)

For the Place Setting Card, measuring 9cm x 4cm (3½in x 1½in):

5cm (2in) square of 22-count Hardanger fabric
Stranded embroidery cotton in the colours given in the panel
No26 tapestry needle
Card, obtainable from specialist suppliers (see page 256)

●

PLACEMAT AND NAPKIN

For the placemat, mark the central horizontal line across the fabric with a line of basting stitches. From the left-hand side of the fabric, measure in along this line for 10cm (4in). A vertical line at this point marks the centre, from which you should start your embroidered panel, which is made up of two motifs, one on each side of the horizontal line.

For the napkin, which features only one motif, baste a vertical line 10cm (4in) in from the left

hand side and a horizontal one 13.5cm (5¼in) up from the lower edge. The centre of the motif is the point where these two lines intersect.

For both the placemat and the napkin, use three strands of embroidery cotton in the needle for the cross stitch and the backstitching of the stems. Use only two threads in the needle for backstitching the fine detail on the flower centre and petals. Work over two fabric threads.

Gently steam press the finished embroideries on the reverse side.

FRINGING

Trim around the finished embroideries, so that the placemat measures 46cm x 34cm (18½in x 13½in) and the napkin measures 37cm (14½in) square.

On all four sides, withdraw a single fabric thread 12mm (½in) in from the outer edge.

The fringing can be secured in one of several ways; by machining around the rectangle (placemat) or square (napkin) left by the withdrawn threads, using either straight stitch or narrow zigzag stitch, or by overcasting every alternate thread by hand.

When you have secured the line, remove all cross threads below the stitched line to complete the fringe. If a more hard-wearing edge is preferred, a hemstitched hem can be used instead of fringing.

PLACE SETTING CARD

Find the centre of the small square of Hardanger, and use one strand of embroidery cotton, to work a single periwinkle. Press on the reverse side. Mount, following the manufacturer's instructions.

▶ PERIWINKLE	DMC	ANCHOR	MADEIRA
• Pale mauve	211	342	0801
◥ Yellow	726	295	0109
⊏ Dark green	3363	262	1602
⊆ Green	3347	266	1408
⊔ Bright green	989	242	1401
÷ Pale green	3364	260	1603
⊐ Dark purple	550	102	0714
Ⅱ Purple	208	110	0804
△ Dark mauve	209	109	0803
⊐ Mauve	210	108	0802
White*	Blanc	White	White

Note: Backstitch stems in pale green, flower centres in dark green, and flower petals in white* (used for backstitch only).

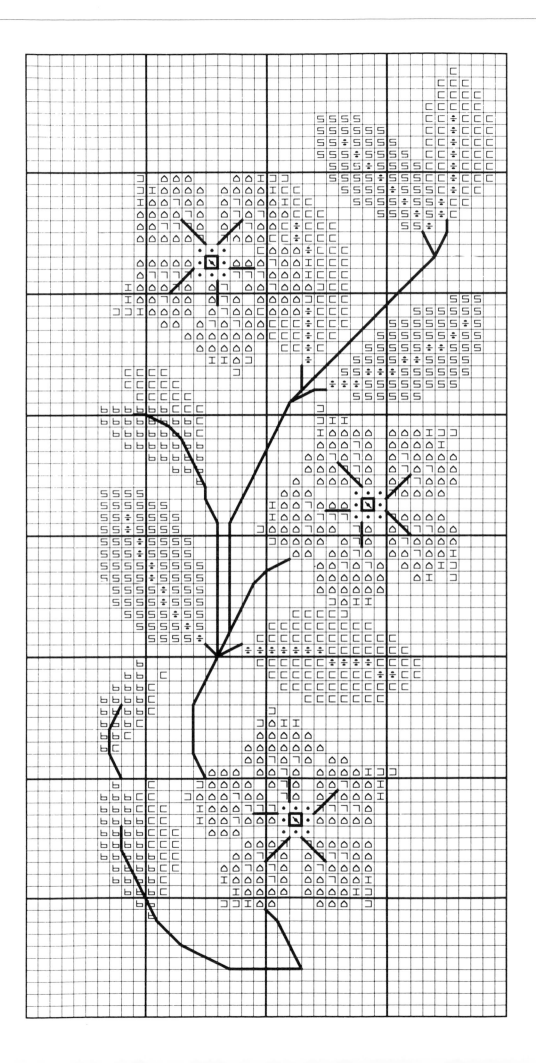

SUMMER SPICE

YOU WILL NEED

For the Picture, set in a frame with an internal measurement
of 35cm x 30cm (14in x 12in):

*45.5cm x 40.5cm (18in x 16in) of emerald green,
14-count Aida fabric
Stranded embroidery rayon and cotton in the colours listed
No26 tapestry needle
Frame, as specified above
Firm card (for the embroidery to be laced over)
to fit the frame
Wadding (batting) to fit the frame
Two cardboard mounts to fit the frame, one with a
22.5cm x 17.5cm (9in x 7in) aperture, and one with a
23cm x 18cm (9¼in x 7¼in) aperture
Glue stick*

•

THE EMBROIDERY

Prepare the fabric (see *Basic Skills* pages 8–11): find the centre by folding the fabric in half and then in half again, and lightly pressing the corner, or by marking the horizontal and vertical centre lines with basting stitches in a light-coloured thread. Mount the fabric in a frame (see *Basic Skills* pages 8–11) and start the design from the centre.

Following the chart, complete all the cross stitching first, using three strands of thread in the needle. Where two colours are given for a symbol be careful to check that you are using the correct colours and thread types. Finally, long stitch stems, using two strands of light green in the needle.

FINISHING

Remove the embroidery from the frame and wash if necessary, then steam press lightly on the wrong side. Spread glue evenly on one side of the mounting card, and lightly press the wadding to the surface. Lace the embroidery over the padded surface (see *Basic Skills* pages 8–11), using the basting stitches (if any) to check that it is centred over the card.

Remove basting stitches; place the cardboard mounts and the embroidery in the frame, and assemble according to the manufacturer's instructions.

COMPLETE THREAD LIST
STRANDED EMBROIDERY COTTON

	ANCHOR	DMC	MADEIRA
Silver green	875	966	1702
Light green	255	907	1410
Medium green	257	905	1411
Yellow	298	972	0107
Mustard	306	783	0114
Orange red	332	608	0206
Medium red	19	347	0211
Deep red	20	498	0513
Violet	101	552	0713
BROWN	381	938	2005

STRANDED RAYON THREAD

	Lorem
Gold	821
Orange	850
Red	843
Pink	813
Lilac	858
Purple	859

SUMMER SPICE		ANCHOR	DMC	MADEIRA
▬	Silver green	875	966	1702
I	Light green	255	907	1410
II	Medium green	257	905	1411
↓	Mustard	306	783	0114
X	Dark red	20	498	0513
●	Brown	381	938	2005

Note: For the above symbols, use three strands of cotton in the needle. Straight stitch stems using two strands of light green.

MARLITT

⬉	Pink	813

Note: For the above symbol use three strands of rayon in the needle.

		MAR/ANC	MAR/DMC	MAR/MAD
+	Gold/yellow	821/298	821/972	821/0107
O	Orange/orange red	850/332	850/608	850/0206
V	Red/medium red	843/19	843/347	8430211
□	Lilac/violet	858/101	859/552	858/0713
■	Purple/violet	859/101	859/552	859/0713

Note: For the above symbols, use two strands of rayon with one strand of cotton.

		MAR/ANC	MAR/DMC	MAR/MAD
⋮⋮	Red/orange red	843/332	843/608	843/0206

Note: For the above symbol use one strand of rayon with two strands of cotton.

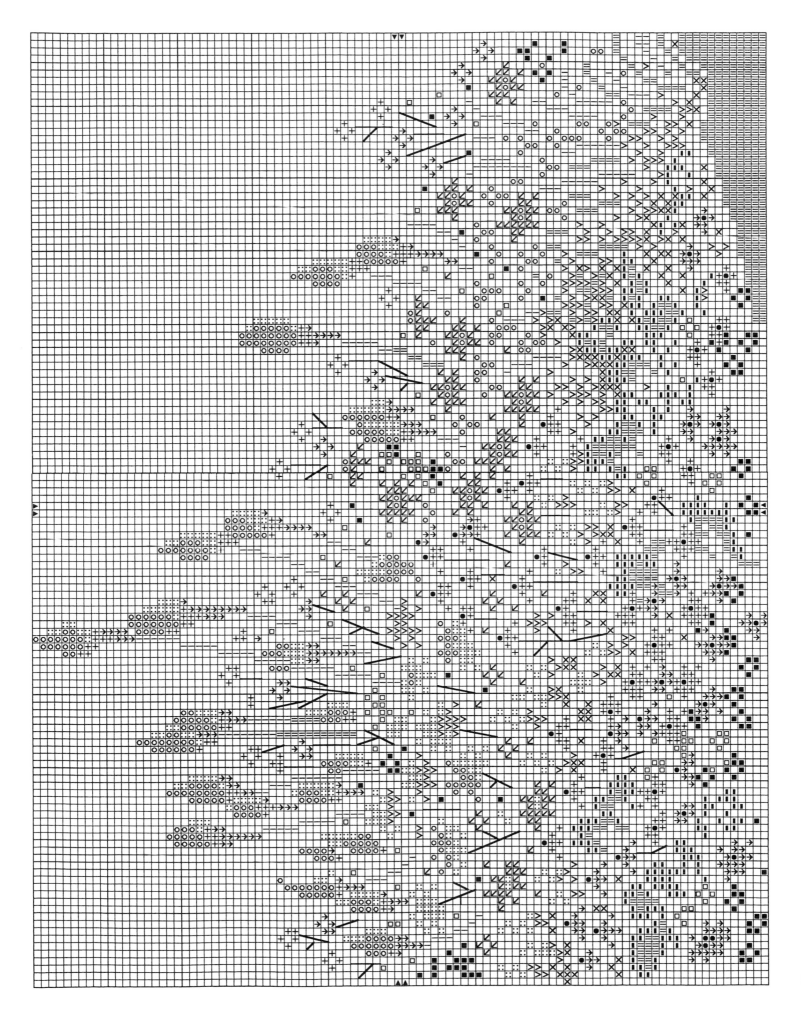

Floral Feast

Once again, a selection of traditional flower motifs have been arranged to create this attractive floral sampler. The pinks in the basket of roses are echoed in the daisy-like flowers at the top of the sampler and complement the mauve shades of the other flowers. By adding your name and the date the sampler was worked, you can create an heirloom for future generations!

FLORAL FEAST

YOU WILL NEED

For the Floral Feast Sampler, with a design area measuring 18.5cm x 21cm (7½in x 8¼in), or 101 stitches by 119 stitches, here in a frame measuring 31cm x 35cm (12¼in x 14in):

28.5cm x 31cm (11½in x 12¼in) of Zweigart's white, 14-count Aida fabric
Stranded embroidery cotton in the colours given in the panel
No24 tapestry needle
Strong thread, for lacing across the back
Cardboard, for mounting, sufficient to fit into the frame recess
Frame of your choice

●

THE EMBROIDERY

Prepare the fabric and stretch it in a frame (see *Basic Skills* pages 8–11). Following the appropriate chart, start the embroidery at the centre of the design, using two strands of embroidery cotton in the needle. Work each stitch over one block of fabric in each direction. Make sure that all the top crosses run in the same direction and each row is worked into the same holes as the top or bottom of the row before so that you do not leave a space between the rows. Then embroider your name and the date.

MAKING UP

Gently steam press the work on the reverse side and mount (see *Basic Skills* pages 8–11). As this is a sampler with traditional motifs, it has been framed without a mount so that it is in keeping with the samplers stitched around the turn of the century. The rose motif would look most attractive as a separate picture, and other motifs could also be extracted and used in this manner, perhaps with minor modifications.

▶ FLORAL FEAST		DMC	ANCHOR	MADEIRA
⟨	Light pink	604	60	0614
+	Medium pink	603	63	0701
O	Dark pink	600	65	0704
%	Light mauve	210	108	0803
—	Dark mauve	208	111	0804
V	Yellow	743	301	0113
S	Light green	369	213	1309
=	Medium green	320	215	1311
‡	Dark green	367	217	1312
X	Light brown	729	890	2209
⟩	Dark brown	434	365	2009

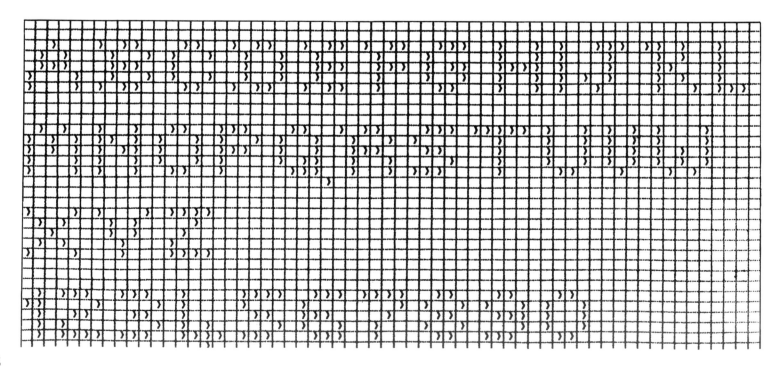

Honeysuckle Beauty

Alphonse Mucha created some of the most stunning Art Nouveau images, many of which are still popular today. Adorned with jewels and flowers, this beautiful design is typical of his decadent style and a challenge to experienced stitchers.

HONEYSUCKLE BEAUTY

YOU WILL NEED

For the Picture, with a design area measuring
19cm x 17.5cm (7½in x 7in):

*35cm (14in) square of pale peach, 28-count
evenweave fabric
Stranded embroidery cotton and specialist thread in the
colours listed in the panel
No26 tapestry needle
Brass charm for hair ornament (optional)
Seed beads in the colours listed in the panel*

*Firm card for backing
Strong thread for lacing
Frame and mount of your choice*

●

THE EMBROIDERY

Prepare the fabric and find the centre point (see *Basic Skills* pages 8–11). Using two strands of thread in the needle (unless indicated in the key), work the cross stitching over two threads of fabric. When stitching with rayon blending filament or metallic braid, see *Basic Skills* pages 8–11. I used part of an old necklace to make the hair ornament but a brass charm would work too. The ornament is suspended from a gold chain which can be completed in chain stitch or backstitch.

▶ HONEYSUCKLE BEAUTY

		DMC	ANCHOR	MADEIRA	MARLITT/ KREINIK
—	White	01	02	2402	–
↓	Gold braid				Kreinik No.8 017HL
⌐	Light purple x 1 plus medium purple x 1	210	108	0802	857
▼	Black	310	403	2400	–
●	Medium brown	434	310	2009	–
⠒	Light brown	436	1045	2011	–
�	Purple x 1 plus medium purple rayon x 1	550	99	0713	858
7	Dark purple x 1 plus medium purple rayon x 1	552	101	0714	858
9	Medium purple x 1 plus medium blue rayon x 1	554	96	0711	857
∴	Medium blue	597	168	1110	
X	Medium blue x 1 plus medium blue rayon x 1	597	168	1110	1053
♡	Blue	598	167	1111	–
R	Reddish brown	632	936	2311	–
▷	Dark gold	680	901	2210	–
/	Ecru	712	926	2101	–
◺	Tangerine	742	303	0114	–
∧	Yellow	744	301	0112	–
+	Pale yellow	745	300	0111	–
÷	Peach	758	9575	2309	–
⊹	Plum x 1	778	968	0808	–
T	Brown	801	359	2007	–
▬	Olive	831	277	2201	–
0	Light olive	833	907	2203	–
	Dark brown*	838	380	2005	–
■	Dark plum x 1 plus cerise rayon x 1	915	1029	0705	863
⋈	Medium peach	945	881	2313	–

		DMC	ANCHOR	MADEIRA	MARLITT/ KREINIK
·	Light peach	951	1010	2308	–
⁄	Light pink	963	73	0503	–
→	Turquoise	964	185	1112	–
↑	Medium aqua	993	186	1201	–
❚❚	Dark peach	3064	260	2312	–
▼	Dark green	3345	268	1406	–
I	Green	3347	266	1408	–
S	Medium pink	3354	74	2610	–
▲	Dark pink x 1 plus cerise rayon x 1	3607	87	0708	863
I	Pink x 1 plus light purple rayon x 1	3609	85	0710	1214
◥	Dark cerise	3721	896	0811	–
⊟	Cerise	3731	76	0506	–
Y	Light cerise	3733	75	0504	–
◁	Light plum x 1	3743	869	2611	–
◇	Light flesh	3770	1009	2314	–
←	Coral	3778	1013	2312	–
K	Dark aqua	3809	169	2507	–
L	Light aqua	3811	928	1002	–
N	Aqua	3814	187	1203	–
⊠	Gold x 1 plus gold blending filament x 1	3820	306	2509	Kreinik Gold 002
⊡	Light gold x 1 plus gold blending filament x 1	3822	295	0112	Kreinik Gold 002
⊒	Cream x 1 plus gold blending filament x 1	3823	386	2511	Kreinik Gold 002
T	Cream	3823	386	2511	
	Deep blue beads	V3.04.930			
	Old gold beads	V3.12.823			

Note: Backstitch end of nose, upper lip and lips in peach; upper and lower eyelids in medium brown; outer edge of gold 'frame' in dark gold; remainder of outlining in dark brown. (*Used for backstitch and straight stitch only.)*

Work the backstitch using one strand of thread. Use one strand of Kreinik gold braid No.8 (017HL) to form the gold fringing on the scarf with straight stitches. Add deep blue beads at the end of each stitch. Using one strand of gold braid, outline the enamelled hair ornament. Using two strands of dark green, stitch the stems of honeysuckle seed heads. Complete the end of each spike in old gold beads.

FINISHING

Remove the finished piece of embroidery from the embroidery frame then press lightly on the wrong side (avoid using steam which can detrimentally affect metallic thread).

Mount and frame your picture (see *Basic Skills* pages 8–11). Alternatively, you could take your project to a professional framer.

VICTORIAN BOUQUET

YOU WILL NEED

For the Picture, with a design size measuring 16cm x 14cm (16⅜in x 5½in):

25cm (10in) square of black, 28-count evenweave linen
Stranded embroidery, cotton and specialist thread in the colours given in the panel
No24 tapestry, needle
Seed beads in the colours given in the panel
Beading needle
Cardboard for mounting, sufficient to fit the frame recess
Strong thread for lacing across the back
Frame of your choice

●

THE EMBROIDERY

Prepare the fabric (see *Basic Skills* pages 8–11). Find the centre and mark the horizontal and vertical lines with basting stitches, then mount the fabric in a frame. Start the embroidery at the centre of the design, using two strands of embroidery thread in the needle. When working the dark mauve stitches, use one strand of dark mauve thread and one strand of blending filament (see *Basic Skills* pages 8–11). Work each stitch over two threads of fabric in each direction, ensuring that all the top crosses run in the same direction and that each row is worked into the same holes as the top or bottom of the row before so that you do not leave a space between the rows. Sew the beads in place.

FINISHING

Remove the finished embroidery from the frame and place it face down on a clean towel. Then gently steam press the work on the reverse side. Mount and frame the embroidery (see *Basic Skills* pages 8–11).

ATTACHING BEADS

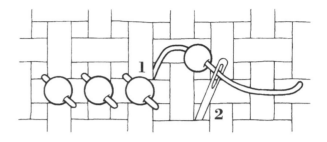

Refer to the chart for bead placement and sew the bead in place using a fine beading needle that will pass through the bead. Bring the needle up at 1, run the needle through the bead, then down at 2. Secure the thread on the back of the work, or move on to the next bead as shown in the diagram.

▶ FLORAL BOUQUET

		DMC	ANCHOR	MADEIRA	KREINIK
☑	Grey	415	398	1803	–
+	Light mauve	553	98	712	–
◩	Dark green	580	924	1608	–
⧉	Green	581	280	1609	–
▼	Very dark green	731	281	1613	–
◇	Light green	733	279	1611	–
╱	Dark mauve x 1 plus dark mauve blending filament x 1	3746	–	0804	012
⠿	Navy blue beads	04.791	–	–	–
⊟	Yellow beads	06.307	–	–	–
⊡	Pearl beads	10.blanc	–	–	–

Note: One pack of beads in each colour is required.

Summer Roses

This bouquet of peach and pink roses is just as fresh as the moment it was picked on a balmy summer's day. The subtle shades of the roses make this picture an ideal focal point for anyone fond of pastel shades. Alternatively, you might choose to embroider the roses in shades of dark pink and red to give warmth and vibrance to the design. The design has been shown here as a picture, but you could, of course, make it into a cushion cover.

SUMMER ROSES

YOU WILL NEED

For the Summer Roses, with a design area measuring 19cm (7½in) square, or 110 stitches by 108 stitches, here in a frame 36cm (14½in) square:

29cm (11½in) of Zweigart's white,
14-count Aida fabric
Stranded embroidery cotton in the colours
given in the panel
No24 tapestry needle
Strong thread, for lacing across the back
Cardboard, for mounting, sufficient to
fit into the frame recess
Frame and mount of your choice.

●

THE EMBROIDERY

Prepare the fabric and stretch it in a frame (see *Basic Skills* pages 8–11). Start at the centre of the design, using two strands of embroidery cotton. Work each stitch over one block of fabric in each direction. Make sure that all the top crosses run in the same direction and each row is worked into the same holes as the top or bottom of the row before, so that you do not leave a space between the rows.

MAKING UP

Steam press on the reverse side and mount (see *Basic Skills* pages 9–11).

▲ SUMMER PICTURE		DMC	ANCHOR	MADEIRA
‡	Light pink	3689	66	0606
/	Medium pink	3688	68	0605
r	Dark pink	3687	69	0604
e	Darkest pink	3685	70	0514
%	Light peach	948	778	0306
a	Medium peach	754	868	0305
o	Dark peach	353	6	0304
n	Darkest peach	352	9	0303
C	Light green	3348	264	1409
X	Medium green	3347	266	1408
=	Dark green	937	268	1504
S	Light brown	950	882	2309
@	Dark brown	407	914	2312

219

Botanical Roses

Look through a text book on roses and,
alongside the more familiar names of
your favourite species, you will find their
scientific names. In this design, the
Latin names have been used as a frame
for the beautiful blooms of a selection of
more traditional roses. Set in a frame
with an appropriate period air, this
beautiful sampler will make an attractive
focal point in any room.

Ribbons and Roses

This picture is an ideal gift for a romantic occasion, such as a wedding or an anniversary. The design could include initials or a date, and the more adventurous stitcher could change the colour of the roses to suit the occasion.

RIBBONS AND ROSES

YOU WILL NEED

For the Rose Picture, mounted in a wooden frame with a 25cm x 30cm (10in x 12in) aperture, with a coloured mount with a 17.5cm x 22.5cm (7in x 9in) aperture:

45.5cm x 38cm (18in x 15in) of 28-count Quaker cloth, in cream
Stranded embroidery cotton in the colours given in the panel
No26 tapestry needle
Strong thread for lacing across the back when mounting
Coloured mount to fit the frame, with an aperture as specified above
Stiff acid-free cardboard, to fit the frame recess
Frame of your choice, with an aperture as specified above
2oz polyester wadding (optional), the same size as the frame aperture, to insert between the embroidery and the cardboard to give slightly padded effect to the framed picture

●

THE EMBROIDERY

Prepare the fabric (see *Basic Skills* pages 8–11), marking the centre lines with basting stitches. Set the fabric in a hoop or frame (see *Basic Skills* pages 8–11) and, starting from a convenient point (such as the centre of the bow), embroider the cross stitches with two strands of stranded cotton. Finish with the backstitching, using one strand. Steam press the finished embroidery on the reverse side.

FRAMING THE PICTURE

For a slightly padded effect, cut a piece of wadding to the exact size of the aperture of the mount; place in the centre of the backing cardboard and, if necessary, fix it with a dab of adhesive at each corner. Lace the embroidery over the cardboard, following the instructions for mounting (see right). Insert the mount and then the mounted embroidery into the frame. Finally, assemble the frame according to the manufacturer's instructions.

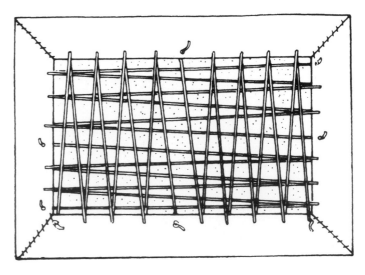

MOUNTING EMBROIDERY

Lay the embroidery face down, with the cardboard centred on top; fold over the edges of the fabric on opposite sides, making mitred folds at the corners, and lace across, using strong thread. Repeat on the other two sides. Finally, pull up the fabric firmly over the cardboard. Overstitch the mitred corners. This method is suitable for larger pictures and heavier fabrics; for lightweight fabrics and smaller embroideries (see *Basic Skills* pages 8–11).

		DMC	ANCHOR	MADEIRA
H	Bright red	321	47	0510
▪▪	Dark red	815	43	0513
▽	Leaf green	905	258	1413
⊐	Bright green	906	256	1411
⊙	Apple green	907	255	1410
▼	Dark green	986	246	1404
⊼	Light red	3801	335	0209
	Very dark red*	902	897	0811

▶ RIBBONS AND ROSES

*Note: Backstitch bow outline with very dark red (*used for backstitching only) and stems of leaves and buds with dark green.*

Floral Alphabet

The treatment of traditional motifs and an alphabet in pastel colours bring this sampler up to date. The border of carnations can easily be extended to make space for your own words underneath the alphabet, or perhaps you could use the space filled here by the letters of the alphabet to write your own message. This sampler can easily be adapted by using alternative shades of cotton. You might choose the opulence of rich, deeper shades, for example, or select colours to match your decor.

FLORAL ALPHABET

YOU WILL NEED

For the Bordered Alphabet sampler, with a design area measuring 26cm x 15cm (10¼in x 6in), or 144 stitches by 85 stitches, here in a frame measuring 36cm x 25cm (14½in x 10in):

36cm x 25cm (14in x 10in) of Zweigart's cream, 14-count Aida fabric
Stranded embroidery cotton in the colours given in the panel
No24 tapestry needle
Strong thread, for lacing across the back
Cardboard for mounting, sufficient to fit into the frame recess
Frame of your choice

●

THE EMBROIDERY

Prepare the fabric and stretch it in a frame (see *Basic Skills* pages 8–11). Following the chart, start the embroidery at the centre of the design, using two strands of embroidery cotton in the needle. Work each stitch over one block of fabric in each direction. Make sure that all the top crosses run in the same direction and that each row is worked into the same holes as the top or bottom of the row before so that you do not leave a space between the rows.

MAKING UP

Steam press the work on the reverse side and mount (see *Basic Skills* pages 8–11). Choose a mount and frame to complement your embroidery colours.

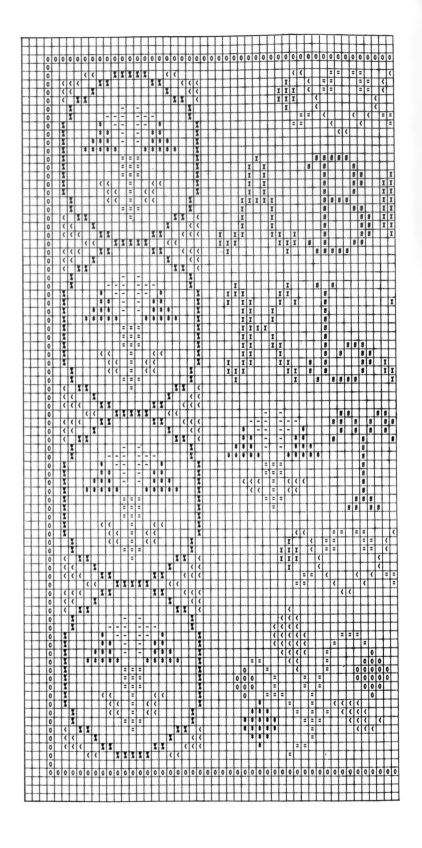

▶ BORDERED ALPHABET			
	DMC	ANCHOR	MADEIRA
‡ Light pink	3689	66	0606
— Dark pink	3688	68	0605
O Pale magenta	3609	85	0710
S Light mauve	211	108	0801
X Dark mauve	210	109	0803
‹ Light green	369	213	1309
= Dark green	368	214	1310
% Brown	841	378	1911

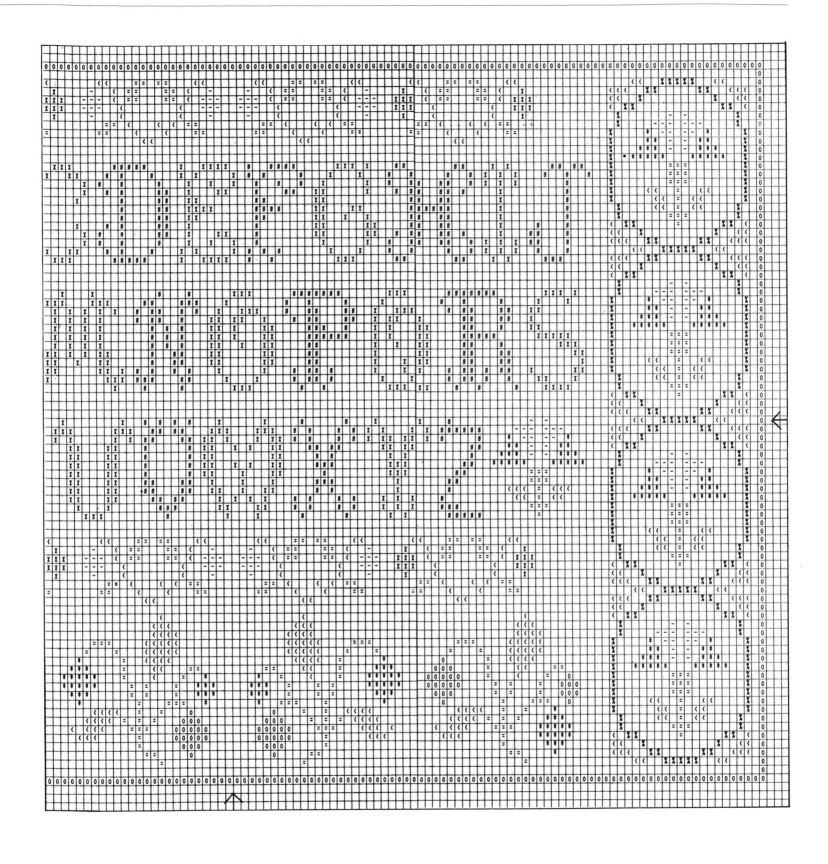

Village Garden

This charming design shows a variety of cottage styles set in a village high street in spring. The cottages are complemented by delicate pink blossom on the trees, and front gardens full of colourful flowers.

VILLAGE GARDEN

YOU WILL NEED

For the Picture, with a design area of
21.5cm x 8.5cm (8¼in x 3½in):

41cm x 29cm (16¼in x 11½in) of light blue,
28-count evenweave fabric
Stranded embroidery cotton in the colours given
in the panel
No24 and No26 tapestry needles
Strong thread for lacing across the back
Cardboard for mounting
Frame of your choice

THE EMBROIDERY

Prepare the fabric, basting the horizontal and vertical lines, (see *Basic Skills* pages 8–11). Set in a hoop or frame, and begin stitching from the centre. Ensure that the long axis of the fabric is running horizontally.

Work the cross stitch over two threads of fabric using two strands of thread in the No24 tapestry needle. Make sure that all the top stitches run in the same direction. Work the backstitch details using one strand of cotton in the No26 needle.

FINISHING

Remove from the frame, and hand wash if desired. Steam press on the reverse side. Mount as shown in *Basic Skills* pp 8–11, following the instructions for heavier fabrics. Frame the mounted picture according to the manufacturer's instructions.

▼ VILLAGE GARDEN

		ANCHOR	DMC	MADEIRA
E	Grey	398	318	1802
L	Cream	386	3823	0102
H	Pale pink	893	225	0814
T	Maroon	44	814	0514
2	Light pink	882	3773	2313
↑	Dark brick	883	3064	2312
3	Rust	349	301	2306
0	Dark emerald green	210	562	1206
·	Emerald green	208	912	1207
=	Bright brown	357	975	2304
N	Light brown	370	434	2303
▼	Light sand	373	3828	2102
S	Dark sand	374	420	2103
Y	Pine green	217	319	1313
+	Dark pine green	218	890	1314

		ANCHOR	DMC	MADEIRA
▽	Purple	110	209	0803
K	Dark brown	1050	3781	1913
←	Light yellow	293	727	0110
⌐	Bright yellow	295	726	0100
∧	Pink	49	818	0404
Z	Black	403	310	Black
/	Grey blue	850	926	1707
V	Grass green	261	3052	1401
⌐	Grey^	398	318	1802
\	Grey*	398	318	1802

Note: Backstitch window details of second house on left with cream. Backstitch window details of third house from left with black. Backstitch all other details with dark brown. Work grey^ in cross stitch with one strand. Work grey in tent stitch with one strand.*

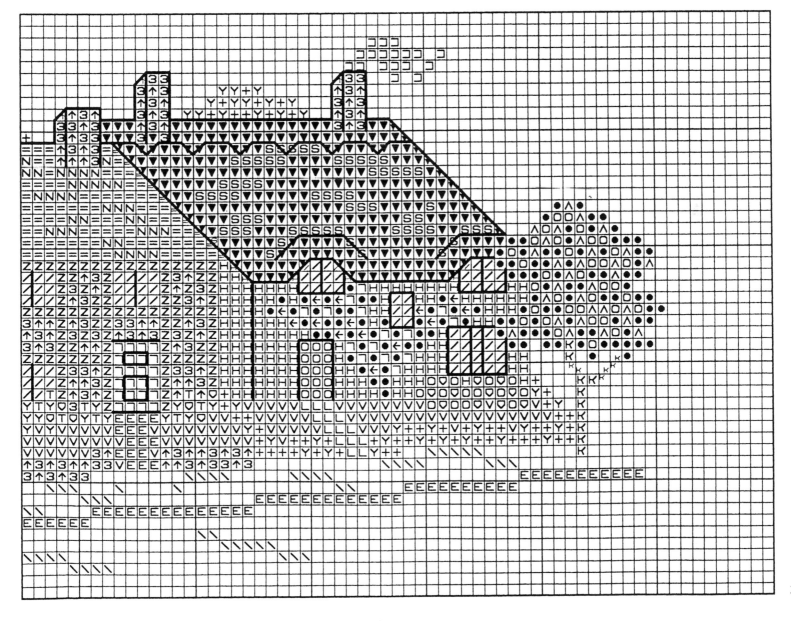

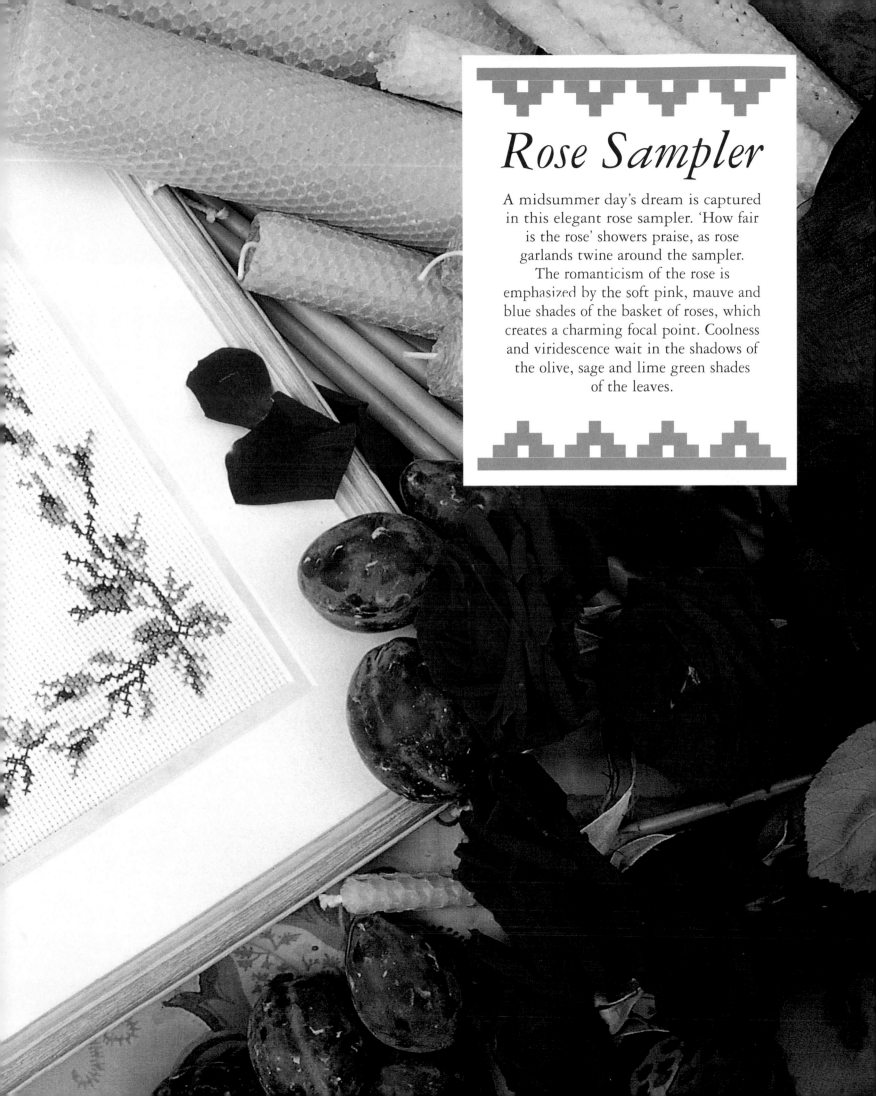

Rose Sampler

A midsummer day's dream is captured in this elegant rose sampler. 'How fair is the rose' showers praise, as rose garlands twine around the sampler. The romanticism of the rose is emphasized by the soft pink, mauve and blue shades of the basket of roses, which creates a charming focal point. Coolness and viridescence wait in the shadows of the olive, sage and lime green shades of the leaves.

ROSE SAMPLER

YOU WILL NEED

For the Sampler with a design area measuring
26.5cm x 31cm (10½in x 12¼in), or 154 stitches
by 175 stitches, here in a frame measuring
42.5cm x 46cm (17in x 18½in):

*36.5cm x 41cm (14½in x 16½in) of Zweigart's
white, 14-count Aida fabric
Stranded embroidery cotton in the colours given
in the panel
No24 tapestry needle
Strong thread for lacing across the back
Cardboard for mounting, sufficient to fit in to
the frame recess
Frame of your choice*

●

THE EMBROIDERY

Prepare the fabric and stretch it in a frame (see
Basic Skills pages 8–11). Following the chart, start
the embroidery at the centre of the design, using
two strands of embroidery cotton in the needle.
Work each stitch over one block of fabric in each
direction. Make sure that all the top crosses run in
the same direction and each row is worked into the
same holes as the top or bottom of the row before,
so that you do not leave a space between the rows.

To give the basket more definition, work the
outline in backstitch, with one strand of darkest
brown cotton in the needle.

The shades chosen would fit very well in a bedroom colour scheme, but the sampler would look
equally attractive if the colours were changed for
stronger shades of green for the leaves and perhaps
red and dark magenta for the roses.

MAKING UP

Gently steam press the work on the reverse side and
mount (see *Basic Skills* pages 8–11). When framing
the picture, consider using a double mount with
the darker of the shades on the inside, to give
your sampler extra depth. Do not prepare your
embroidery by lacing it over the mounting
cardboard until you have chosen your frame and
decided whether you will also require a mount
(double or single). These decisions will all affect
the amount of fabric that you will wish to leave
around the edges of the embroidered area.

	► ROSE SAMPLER	DMC	ANCHOR	MADEIRA
/	Light pink	3689	66	0606
:	Medium pink	3688	68	0605
<	Dark pink	3685	70	0514
>	Light mauve	211	342	0801
\	Medium mauve	210	109	0803
C	Dark mauve	208	111	0804
V	Yellow	3078	292	0102
‡	Light blue	932	920	0907
+	Dark blue	311	148	1007
O	Light green	369	213	1309
r	Medium green	320	215	1311
S	Dark green	319	217	1313
W	Light brown	842	376	1910
X	Medium brown	841	378	1911
Z	Dark brown	840	379	1912
	Darkest brown*	938	381	2005

*Darkest brown used for backstitch outline of basket only.

United in Marriage

This band sampler is simple but very effective. You may like to alter the colours to match the bridesmaids' dresses or the wedding bouquets. The powder compact could be a gift from the bride to a bridesmaid.

UNITED IN MARRIAGE

YOU WILL NEED

For the Sampler, set in a frame with an external measurement of 26cm x 41.5cm (10¼in x 16in) and a double mount with an aperture measuring 14cm x 29cm (5¾in x 11⅜in):

28cm x 41.5cm (11in x 16½in) of 28-count Annabelle fabric, in blue/grey
Stranded embroidery cotton in the colours given in the appropriate panel
No26 tapestry needle
Mount(s) with an aperture as specified above
Frame of your choice
Strong thread, for lacing across the back when mounting
Stiff cardboard, cut to fit inside the frame recess, for mounting

Note: To add to the effect, two mounts have been used – a cream mount, with an aperture as specified above, and a blue mount, with an aperture 1cm (½in) larger each way, to reveal the cream mount.

For the Powder Compact with an inset measuring 6.5cm (2¼in) in diameter

12.5cm (5in) square of 28-count Jobelan fabric, in antique white
Stranded embroidery cotton in the colours given in the appropriate panel
No26 tapestry needle
Powder compact (for suppliers see page 256)

●

THE EMBROIDERY

For the sampler, prepare the fabric (see *Basic Skills* pages 8–11), marking the centre with horizontal and vertical lines of basting stitches. Set the fabric in a hoop or frame (see *Basic Skills* pages 8–11) then, following the chart, start from the centre and work outwards. Use two strands of embroidery cotton for the cross stitches, making sure each stitch covers two threads of the fabric. Finish with backstitching, using two strands of embroidery cotton.

For the powder compact, prepare the fabric (see *Basic Skills* pages 8–11). Beginning from the centre of the chart, embroider the motif, using two strands of embroidery cotton and making sure each cross stitch covers two threads of fabric.

Hand wash the finished embroideries, if necessary, and press gently on the reverse side with a steam iron.

ASSEMBLY

Using the basting stitches as guidelines, centre the sampler over the cardboard mount, which should have been cut to fit the chosen frame. Lace the embroidery over the mount (see *Basic Skills* pages 8–11). When you have finished, gently remove the basting stitches from the piece. Then place the two mounts and the mounted embroidery into the frame, and complete assembly, according to the manufacturer's instructions.

For the powder compact, use the template provided with the compact to trim the fabric to fit the lid inset (you may find it easier to keep the design centred if you leave the basting stitches in position until the fabric has been trimmed to shape). Complete assembly, following the manufacturer's instructions.

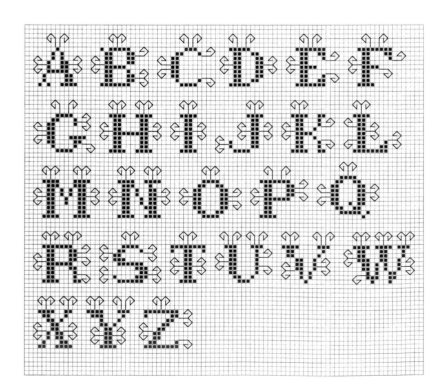

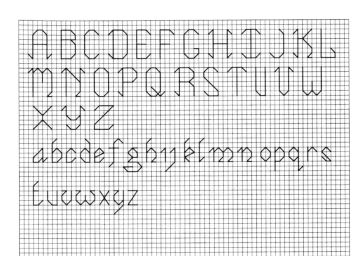

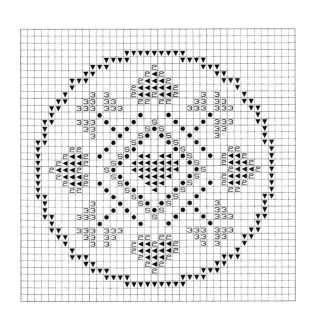

Golden Lace Fan

Emulate the Victorian era with this lace-effect fan, decorated with sprigs of violets and richly embellished with gold thread. This design is stitched on antique white Aida fabric, but you could use plastic canvas and trim it into a fan shape if you prefer.

GOLDEN LACE FAN

YOU WILL NEED

For the Picture, with a design size measuring
22.5cm x 14cm (9in x 5½in):

*32.5cm x 24cm (13in x 9½in) of antique white,
14-count Aida fabric
Stranded embroidery cotton and specialist thread in the
colours given in the panel
No24 tapestry needle
Cardboard for mounting, sufficient to fit the
frame recess
Strong thread for lacing across the back
Mount and frame of your choice*

•

THE EMBROIDERY

Prepare the fabric and stretch it in a frame (see
Basic Skills pages 8–11). Find the centre of the
design and mark the central horizontal and vertical
lines on the fabric with basting stitches. Following
the chart, start the embroidery at the centre of the
design using two strands of embroidery thread in
the needle, except when using brown thread, when
only one strand should be used. Work each cross
stitch over one block of fabric in each direction.
Make sure that all the top crosses run in the same
direction and that each row is worked into the top
or bottom of the row before so that you do not leave
a space between the rows. Work the backstitch
using one strand of thread in the needle.

FINISHING

Remove the completed embroidery from the
frame, and wash, if necessary. Then place the
embroidery face down on a clean towel, and gently
steam press. Mount and frame the embroidery (see
Basic Skills pages 8–11).

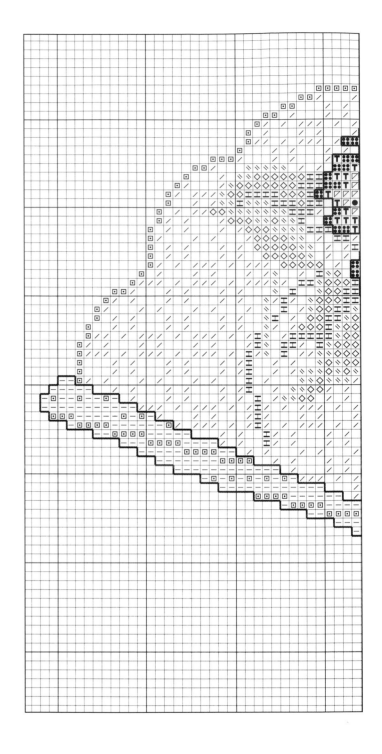

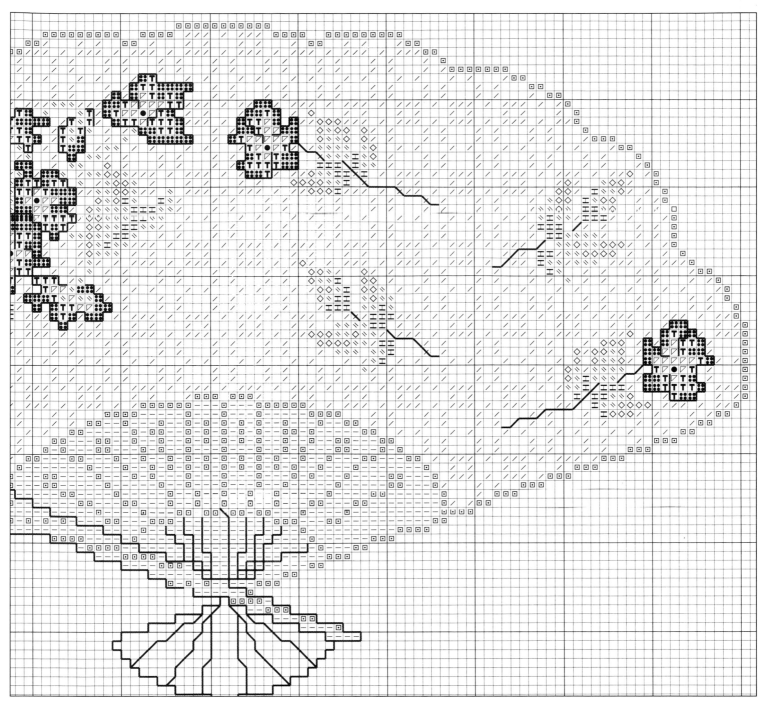

		DMC	ANCHOR	MADEIRA
T	Dark mauve	340	118	0902
⠆	Mauve	341	117	0901
●	Yellow	727	293	0110
—	Cream	746	275	2101
/	Brown (1 strand only)	841	378	1911
I	Dark green	3345	268	1504
\	Green	3347	266	1502
◇	Light green	3348	264	1501
◺	Light mauve	3747	117	0901
▣	Gold	4024	—	—

Note: Backstitch outlines in dark green.

Rose Cottage

Walk down the pathway of this English cottage garden and take a step back in time. In your imagination, smell the scent of lavender and absorb the colours and peacefulness of a bygone era. The rambling roses around the cottage door are embroidered with clusters of French knots to give extra depth and texture to this nostalgic design. It has been set in a deep frame, but an alternative idea would be to surround it with a double mount, to add to the sense of perspective.

ROSE COTTAGE

YOU WILL NEED

For the Rose Cottage, with a design area measuring 19.5cm x 15cm (7¾in x 6in), or 119 stitches by 85 stitches, here in a frame measuring 23cm x 18.5cm (9in x 7½in):

30cm x 25cm (12in x 10in) of Zweigart's white, 14-count Aida fabric
Stranded embroidery cotton in the colours given in the panel
No24 tapestry needle
Strong thread, for lacing across the back
Cardboard for mounting, sufficient to fit in the frame recess
Frame and mount of your choice

●

THE EMBROIDERY

Prepare the piece of fabric and stretch it in a frame (see *Basic Skills* pages 8–11). Following the chart, start the embroidery at the centre of the design, using two strands of embroidery cotton in the needle. Work each stitch over a block of fabric in each direction. Make sure that all the top crosses run in the same direction and each row is worked into the same holes as the top or bottom of the row before, so that you do not leave a space between the rows.

Using backstitch, work all the outlines and markings with one strand of dark green cotton. Work the roses in clusters of medium and dark coloured pink French knots, using six strands of cotton in the needle and winding the cotton around the needle either once or twice, varying this so that some clusters of roses stand out more than others, to create a three-dimensional effect.

ROSE COTTAGE		DMC	ANCHOR	MADEIRA			DMC	ANCHOR	MADEIRA
/	Light pink	776	73	0606	C	Cream	746	275	0101
:	Medium pink	894	26	0408	+	Light gold	676	887	2208
<	Dark pink	891	29	0412	n	Medium gold	729	890	2209
\	Light mauve	210	108	0803	g	Dark gold	680	901	2210
>	Medium mauve	208	111	0804	V	Yellow	743	301	0113
%	Dark mauve	550	101	0714	‡	Light blue	799	130	0910

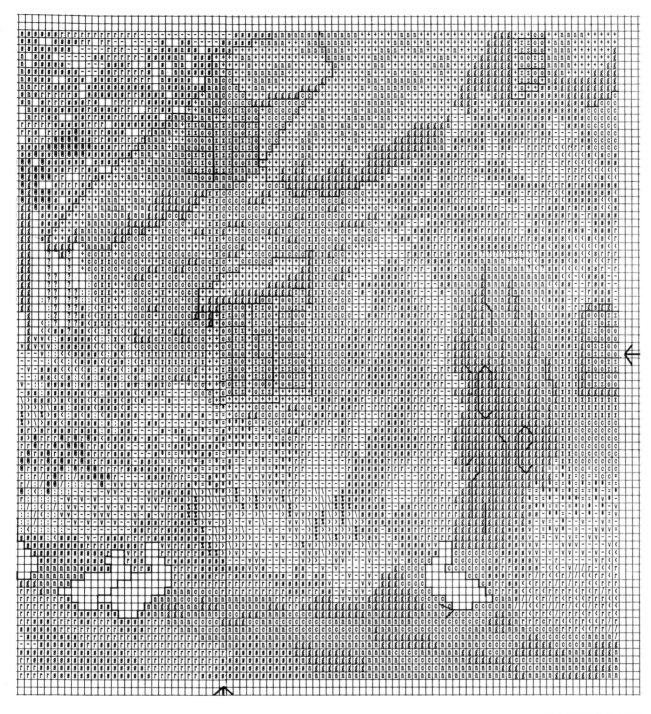

MAKING UP

Steam press the work on the reverse side and mount (see *Basic Skills* pages 8–11). Choose a mount and frame that are in keeping with the 'Olde Worlde' charm of the picture.

		DMC	ANCHOR	MADEIRA
=	Dark blue	798	131	0911
−	Light green	3348	264	1409
Γ	Medium green	3347	266	1408
S	Dark green	3345	268	1406
@	Darkest green	936	263	1507
X	Light brown	434	365	2009

		DMC	ANCHOR	MADEIRA
?	Dark brown	829	906	2106
O	Light grey	762	234	1804
Z	Dark grey	414	399	1801

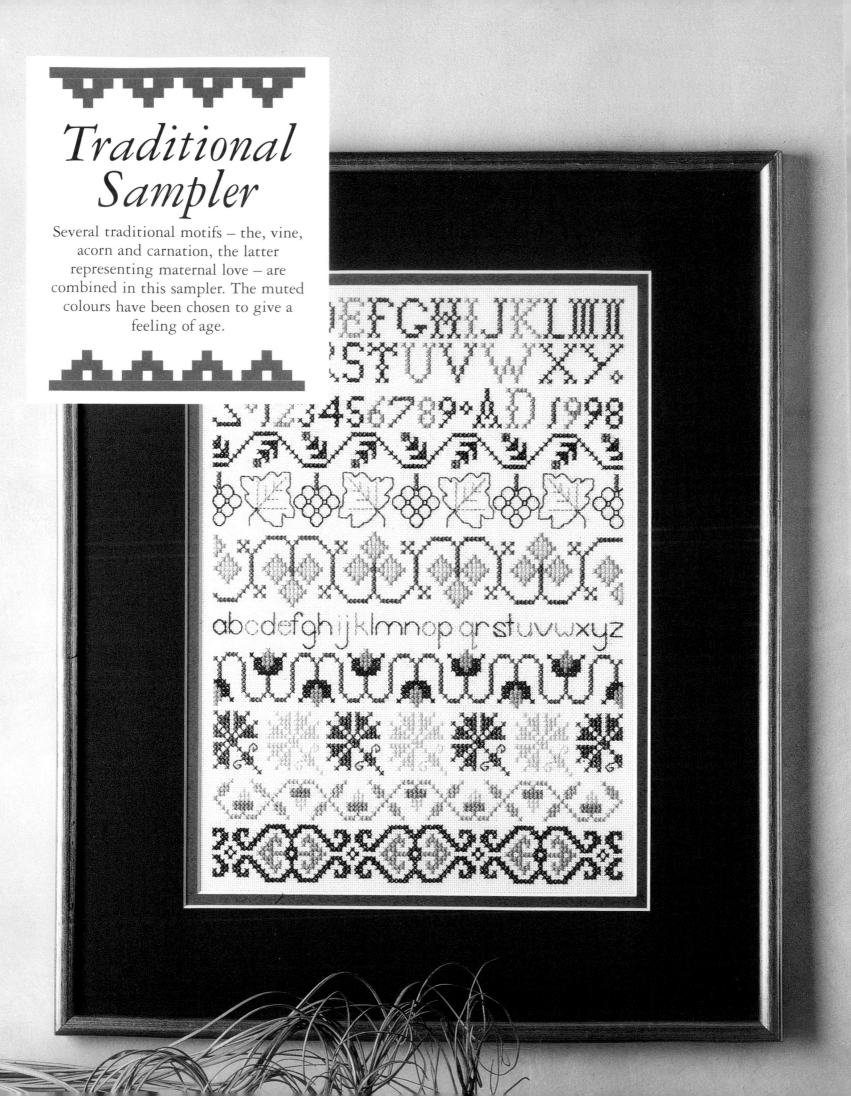

Traditional Sampler

Several traditional motifs – the, vine, acorn and carnation, the latter representing maternal love – are combined in this sampler. The muted colours have been chosen to give a feeling of age.

TRADITIONAL SAMPLER

YOU WILL NEED

For the Sampler, set in a frame with an external measurement of 34.5cm x 42cm (13½in x 16½in), and a double mount with an aperture measuring 20.5cm x 28.5cm (8¼in x 11¼in):

33cm x 39.5cm (13in x 15½in) of 28-count Jobelan fabric, in bone
Stranded embroidery cotton in the colours given in the appropriate panel
No26 tapestry needle
Frame and mounts of your choice
Strong thread for lacing across the back when mounting
Stiff cardboard, cut to fit inside the frame recess, for mounting

Note: To add to the effect, two mounts have been used – a dark blue mount, with an aperture as specified above, and a maroon mount, with an aperture 1cm (½in) larger each way, to reveal the blue mount.

An alternative variation would be to focus on a single design element from the sampler, such as the acorn motif, and use this for smaller items, such as greeting cards or gift tags.

THE EMBROIDERY

First prepare the fabric (see *Basic Skills* pages 8–11), marking the centre both ways with horizontal and vertical lines of basting stitches. Set the fabric in a hoop or frame (see *Basic Skills* pages 8–11) and work out from the centre, completing all cross stitches first and using two strands of embroidery cotton. Ensure each cross stitch covers two threads of fabric. Finish with the backstitches, this time using one strand of embroidery cotton. When stitching is complete, hand wash the embroidery if necessary and press gently on the reverse side.

ASSEMBLY

Using the basting stitches as guidelines, centre the sampler over the cardboard mount. Lace the embroidery over the mount (see *Basic Skills* pages 8–11) . When you have finished, gently remove the basting stitches. Place the two mounts and then the mounted embroidery into the frame, and complete assembly, according to the manufacturer's instructions.

abcdefghljklmnop qrstuvwxyz

▲ TRADITIONAL SAMPLER

		DMC	ANCHOR	MADEIRA
1	Dark grey green	520	862	1505
2	Light grey green	522	860	1513
−	Dark gold	680	901	2210
3	Dark red	814	45	0514
X	Brown	838	380	1914

		DMC	ANCHOR	MADEIRA
И	Light brown	840	898	1912
/	Very light brown	842	831	1910
8	Blue	930	922	1712
H	Very dark green	934	862	1506
■	Light gold	3046	887	2206

Note: Backstitch vine leaves in light grey green, grapes in dark red, lower case alphabet in same colour sequence as large alphabet, and flower tendrils in the flower colour.

INDEX

SUPPLIERS

UK
Elizabeth R. Anderson
Rosedale, 16 Tall Elms
Close, Bromley
Kent BR2 OTT

Hanging by a Thread
PO Box 10723
London SE3 02L

Impress Cards and Craft
Materials
Slough Farm
Westhall
Halesworth
Suffolk IP19 8RN

S & A Frames
The Old Post Office
Yarra Road
Cleethorpes
North Lincolnshire
DN35 8LS

Craft Creations
Ingersoll House
Delamare Road
Cheshunt
Hertfordshire EN8 9ND

Crafters Pride
Macleod Craft Marketing
West Yonderton
Warlock Road
Bridge of Weir
Renfrewshire PA11 3SR

Quilts and Crafts
4 Allandale Road
Stoneygate, Leicester
LE2 2DA

R.A. and P.A. Bolt
Swiss Cottage
Milton Abbas
Blandford
Dorset DT11 OBJ

Fabric Flair Limited
Unit 3 Northlands
Industrial Estate
Copheap Lane
Warminster
Wiltshire BA12 0BG

Framecraft Miniatures
Limited
372/376 Summer Lane
Hockley
Birmingham, B19 3QA

INTERNATIONAL
Ireland Needlecraft Pty Ltd
PO Box 1175
Nare Warren M.D.C.
Victoria 3805
Australia

Danish Art Needlework
PO Box 442, Lethbridge
Alberta T1J 3Z1
Canada

Sanyei Imports
PO Box 5, Hashima Shi
Gifu 501-62
Japan

The Embroidery Shop
286 Queen Street
Masterton
New Zealand

S. A. Threads and Cottons
Ltd
43 Somerset Road
Cape Town
South Africa

DMC (also distributors
of Zweigart fabrics)

UK
DMC Creative World Ltd
62 Pullman Road,
Wigston
Leicester, LE8 2DY

USA
The DMC Corporation
Port Kearney Bld.
10 South Kearney
N.J. 07032-0650

AUSTRALIA
DMC (Australia) Pty Ltd
PO Box 317
Earlswood
NSW 2206

COATS AND
ANCHOR
(also distributors of
Kreinik blending
filament)

UK
Coats Paton Crafts
McMullen Road,
Darlington
Co. Durham DL1 1YQ

USA
Coats & Clark
PO Box 27067
Dept CO1
Greenville
SC 29616

AUSTRALIA
Coats $pencer Crafts
Private Bag 15
Mulgrave North
Victoria 3170

MADEIRA

UK
Madeira Threads (UK) Ltd
Thirsk Industrial Park
York Road,
Thirsk
N.Yorkshire, Y07 3BX

USA
Madeira Marketing
Limited
600 East 9th Street
Michigan City
IN 46360

AUSTRALIA
Penguin Threads Pty
Limited
25-27 Izett Street
Prahran
Victoria 3181